HOMICIDES IN HARLEM

The Turbulent Stories & Life of a New York City Detective

PAUL MERLINO

Printed in the United States of America
First Printing 2020
First Edition 2020
Second Printing 2021
Second Edition 2021

11 10 9 8 7 6 5 4 3 2

HOMICIDES
IN HARLEM

Introduction

Who is Walt Merlino? What are his tales? When and where did they take place? Good questions, and this journey will take you to my childhood, his childhood, all the way up to me as a young adult. Many of the tales take place in New York City. The tales usually occur from 1950 until 1970. But not always. Sometimes in Florida as well, and certainly while Walt is the key protagonist, he is not the only character, flawed or otherwise, featured in these stories.

The big question and your original question is, "Who is (or was) Walt?" A simple question, isn't it? Yet complicated. He was a pilot during World War II, an instructor, and flew B-17 bombers. He was the only son of a very hard-working Italian-American self-made man. He was the loving son of a German-English eccentric woman who was 30 years old when she finally married.

He was also a postman, New York City policeman, detective, and plainclothesman. Later on in life, he was a cemetery plot salesman, a telephone salesman, and a slightly better than average realtor.

He was a mostly faithful husband of a pretty German-Irish-American woman, June, who was cleverer than she let on and yet self-destructed in pity, disappointment, occasional violence fueled with Bombay gin and Pall Mall cigarettes.

Walt had two sons who first adored him, then feared him. They then graduated to hating and finally loathing him and, at the end, sort of accepted him and possibly pitied him as well. They, his sons, were reasonably successful despite the odds and went on to do bigger and better things again despite negative encouragement, boredom, and physical and emotional violence.

Walt was larger than life; when he was happy, he looked like Jackie Gleeson of the old Honeymooners TV show. Normally, he looked like Carroll O'Connor of All In The Family when talking about the problems facing America in the 1970s. When he ramped up from anger to rage, he summoned a demon that successfully eliminated all light and hope and tried its best to cover his target with the endless depths of torments.

Yet, despite what I just told you, he had a heart bigger than most when a family member, friend, or pet was sick, injured, or somehow threatened by what he perceived as external to the core family.

At parties, he was usually the magnet that drew people to him, an excellent and warm host with reasonably intelligent conversation. He believed in the afterlife and would watch hours of Jimmy Swaggart, a very flawed TV evangelical preacher. Walt couldn't be bothered to attend church. He saw no contradiction in quoting bible verses and yet using unspeakable obscenities about anyone, including his family, who he perceived to have crossed him.

So who is Walt? Well, you may have guessed already, but Walt was my father. I have him to thank and blame for who I am today. A negative role model, you may say. Yet there was a positive aspect about him and that was that Walt excelled in the art of storytelling.

Now I will relay some of his more memorable stories, from the mundane to the spectacular. Ones which he told again and again and rarely could I catch him out with any missed or exaggerated details. Are they true? I think so, certainly where I was a witness or, in some cases, a recipient of Walt's "attention'" However, prepare for this journey into the past with an open mind and heart. The tales I will lay out now, I was told by Walt, and I believed they were true. This both frightens and yet propels me to put these stories to print while I still remember them well.

My younger brother, whose nickname is Roots, and I both spoke in-depth about these stories, and over a period of years, ironed out details of what happened and when these events occurred.

There were three distinct periods of Walt's life that appear in these stories:

1) Growing up in the Bronx during the Great Depression and his life in the US Army Air Corps during World War II,

2) Working as a detective and policeman in New York City between 1950-1970,

3) His largely unsuccessful attempt to resettle in Florida after retirement from the NYPD.

However, from time to time, we heard stories about Walt's parents and grandparents, which added to the puzzle. Stories about his unexpected and bewildering encounters with the paranormal too. We also heard, to a lesser extent, stories about June's parents and grandparents, and these stories are recorded here as well. The intention is to allow the reader to look for clues as to why two seemingly normal and decent people developed into something both sad and ultimately destructive. Their pre-history seems tough but no tougher than the average second or third-generation immigrant to America.

So what happened along the way? Why did he transform from a heroic defender of the public to a tragic domestic figure? What were the triggers that ushered him into a moral and mental decline? What were the seeds to ruin?

Our story begins in New York City in the late 1890s.

Chapter 1

Walt's Mother's Memory of Old New York City in the 1890s

On several occasions, my brother and I heard a tragic tale about our family history, which certainly happened. Yet the devil is in the details, which came out over 70 years after the occurrence. My grandmother, May, Walt's mother, started telling this story but was constantly interrupted by Walt. The events were both sad and tragic, yet it did give me a glimpse of what life looked like in the 1890s, which in itself was fascinating and helped guide me into my lifelong desire to study history.

May was one of four children - three girls, and a boy, born to a German immigrant. According to her, they lived in Harlem in Manhattan. In the 1890s, Harlem was mostly a German middle-class neighborhood and the name itself in Dutch meant "beautiful view," primarily because Harlem overlooks the Hudson River. It was also well situated vis-à-vis the small farms in northern Manhattan and the shops and commerce downtown.

The legend goes, May's father had a butcher shop, and both owned the shop and the residence where they lived. He worked hard, six and a half days per week, and by all accounts was strict. His ambition was to buy land north of New York City in Croton-on-Hudson. Allegedly, he did eventually buy his land, and the plan next was to accumulate cash and move from the City into the country for a better life for the entire family.

May said she remembered men visiting her father and having late night meetings. At times, as a young girl, she was afraid, as there was loud talk, cursing and shouting. This went on for several weeks.

She remembered that her father would normally rise around 4.30 am every morning and go to the cellars to prepare meat for his butcher shop upstairs. One morning, his wife said he got up and went to the cellar but did not open the shop at 7 am. As customers knocked on the door of the residence to complain about the shop being closed, May's mother went into the cellar and found her husband face down in water that pooled on the dirt floor. His head was swollen and there was blood in the water. May's father was dead.

The police from the 28th Precinct came to investigate and found no signs of a break-in. Also, they said the body stunk of whiskey. The police theory was that May's father was drunk and went into the cellar, hit his head on a low beam, and fell down the stairs. Water from a recent rainstorm accumulated in the cellar and he drowned. May's mother told the police that he did not drink and that he was up all night with a group of men from City Hall. The police took no notice and ruled the death accidental.

A few days later, just after May's father's funeral, a lawyer came and said that according to the law firm, May's father was in debt due to his habit of gambling, and his home, business, and land was now being foreclosed. As a woman with four young children, with a grammar school education and no husband, May's mother stood no chance at all against City Hall lawyers. Within days there was a court order to evict the family and they literally were on the street with their suitcases.

May's mother started taking on laundry jobs for her former customers, who helped her with small jobs. May's older sisters and brother found work while she helped her mother wash and fold clothing while living in the cellar of a nearby neighbor who took pity on the family. May's job at age seven was to scrub the outdoors marble stairway of her building and that of neighboring buildings every morning.

Walt said the people who his grandfather crossed were not really from City Hall but Tammany Hall, which was a political machine that was corrupt and controlled the Democratic Party, and hence, New York City politics. He said the land they wanted to control was in Croton and was required for a planned reservoir. As May's father was not interested in selling the land, his death was very convenient for a lot of influential people; hence, it was never properly investigated.

At the end of this story, I asked Walt if he investigated this as a detective. He said it was always better to let "sleeping dogs lie" in

New York City. I saw May was visibly upset telling this story and Walt was also becoming agitated. I too learned to let "sleeping dogs lie."

It was then a good time to ask Walt about his father, Lou, and his relationship with his own father, Antonio. We heard snippets of their successes and failures and wanted to hear a more complete story. This narrative was more uplifting than May's story, but it included some hardships as well.

Chapter 2

Walt's Colorful Grandfather, Antonio, in the Early 1900s

Walt used to tell the story of his father's father, Antonio, fondly. Antonio was born in Italy in the 1870s and, as a young man, traveled to New York City to escape poverty and to forge a better living for his family. Walt told the tale how his grandfather arrived on a ship traveling steerage and arrived in New York to be greeted by an Italian-American policeman and sent to Ellis Island for processing. Antonio could not speak a word of English and needed a translator to complete his paperwork. He, fortunately, was found to be healthy and had enough money in his possession, thanks to his father in Italy, and could be processed off Ellis Island and into New York City proper.

Antonio had no place to live, and no one to sponsor him upon arrival. Walt said that he was quite a gregarious young man and managed to befriend another Italian family and rented floor space to sleep on in a tenement near Mulberry Street in Manhattan's Little Italy, which was a fairly large area in the 1890s. Upon getting the lay of the land and being told there was more cheap labor than needed in the area, he had to think quickly on how to survive. No welfare nor community services existed except for church-run soup kitchens for the destitute.

Antonio was able to beg, borrow, and perhaps steal some pieces of fruit, which he polished and put on a broken wooden box on Mott Street, near where he lived, and sold fruit all day and into the night. His sales helped him pay for his floor space in the massively crowded room, which he shared with two larger families. However, Antonio was not looking just to survive but wanted to bring his young wife, Maria, over from Italy along with his infant son. To do this, he hustled and bought large quantities of cheap fruit and vegetables, starting with apples, tomatoes, and potatoes. He would break these bushels up into individual sizes and sell the better pieces early in the morning, and whatever remained was discounted in the afternoon.

He made a subsistence living. After integrating into the Italian community in lower Manhattan, he was able to obtain various odd jobs such as delivery, packing, and cleaning stores at night. He slept little and spent the bare minimum, as he saved up for passage for Maria and the baby. He would say later in life, "Not a day went by when I did not go to sleep hungry."

Within a year, Antonio was able to rent a stall every week on crowded Mott Street and was able to earn enough to pay for his family's transit ahead of schedule, he proudly told anyone who would listen. Antonio soon was successful enough to stop working odd jobs and focus mainly on being not a good greengrocer but,

"The finest in all of Little Italy!", he told both his son and grandson, Lou and Walt. Soon he had a small apartment nearby and was able to not only live there, but he did not have to take in boarders to make ends meet. He used to smile and tease Walt as a young boy by saying, "The apartment looked so large but so lonely; therefore, Grandma and I had to fill it up with beautiful children, including your father and your aunts and uncles as well."

Antonio was able to navigate the depression of 1907 successfully and was able to rent an entire store just after World War I in 1919. He branched into all types of food, including meat, dairy, fish, and confectioneries, along with his specialty of fresh vegetables and fruit. He sublet the growing store space to include a bakery. Things went from good to better until the Great Depression of 1929. What happened then is that neighbors would come and tell Antonio hardship stories about their husbands, brothers, fathers, etc., losing their jobs. They desperately needed milk for the baby, bread for the children, and occasionally money to pay for a doctor's visit. He lived in the neighborhood for almost 40 years and knew his customers like family. While Antonio's wife, Maria, urged him that he sometimes needed to say NO, he just could not do this. Soon Antonio fell behind with his rent and had trouble paying suppliers. By 1932, he lost his store, which he worked so hard to build.

Antonio shrugged and went back to Mott Street and eked out a living doing what he did 40 years ago, buying vegetables in bulk and renting an outside stall every week to pay his bills and look after his family the best he could.

Walt said angrily, "Weren't you angry that you lost everything, Grandpa?" Antonio gently told Walt, "You come into this world with nothing and leave it with nothing. What matters most is what you do to help your family first and your neighbors second. I was not upset at all, as I knew if I worked hard, I could again support my wife and my boys, who were now old enough to look after themselves."

Walt recounted some stories which he remembered from his Grandfather, Antonio. Apparently, Antonio bought a parrot who loved Grandpa, but while the bird was loving, it was "as dumb as shit." Every day, Antonio would feed the parrot pistachios and the bird would sit on his shoulders for hours just saying, "Hello." During the Great Depression, some of Antonio's sons lost their jobs and moved home until they could find work. As Antonio was out selling fruit and vegetables, the boys (now men) would teach the parrot how to curse. When Antonio came home one day, the parrot screeched, "YOU BASTARD!" It also learned, "YOU SON-OF-A-BITCH." Antonio became angry with his children and said, "Hey, you little bastards! What did you do to my beautiful bird?" The sons would laugh and say, "Look, Papa, you taught the bird how to curse, not us!" They would all then laugh and drink Chianti. Grandma Maria would join them for a chuckle as well.

Unfortunately, the parrot learned more profanity, and during the summer, it would shriek horrible words out of the window, which managed to get the Italian men on the sidewalk riled up. They would then shout obscenities back to the bird. Enough was enough, and regrettably, the parrot was sent to Antonios' sister, who lived with her husband in a rural area of Long Island. When the parrot cursed, they would put a blanket over the cage. Antonio heard the poor bird spent most of its remaining life in darkness under the blanket, as he couldn't help but curse... It just liked profanity. The parrot allegedly lived a long and colorful life on Long Island.

Walt also remembered a time when his father, Lou, took Antonio and Walt fishing upstate at Lake Copake. Lou worked at the post office and had use of the post office car, and they drove upstate very early on Sunday morning. He told his father that he would pack sandwiches for Walt and himself and to bring whatever Antonio wanted to eat. Antonio brought along a huge straw picnic basket and Lou said, "What's in there?" and Antonio said, "Worms for the fish," with a big grin.

Out on the lake about midday, with only a few caught fish, Lou took out two plain ham sandwiches and gave one to Walt. With that, Antonio opened his basket which had a whole roasted chicken, cold meatball sandwiches, spicy sausages with sweet green peppers on fresh Italian bread. Lou said, "How are you going to eat all of that?" and Antonio said, "Young Walt and I can handle this." Walt smiled and greedily ate along with his Grandpa, who also managed to have a bottle of Chianti and glasses in the basket. Finally, after teasing his son, Antonio said, "You need to eat up and join us, or you will faint on the drive back; we did not catch enough fish to sustain you, son." They all laughed and Lou begrudgingly ate, as he did not want to see good food go to waste.

Another story relayed by Walt, which Lou was openly embarrassed about, was that around 1908, Lou wanted to learn how to play the guitar. Antonio agreed to hire a local Italian maestro, Dr. Remnanto, who had a reputation of being an excellent teacher, although his tuition was expensive. Apparently, the teacher was a perfectionist and would always urge Lou to do better, practice harder, and to play musical instruments with his heart as well as his hands. One fine day, just after Lou's 12th birthday, the maestro was haranguing him while he was attempting to play a song. Lou then lost it and stopped playing, stood up, and whacked him over the head, breaking his guitar. Dr. Remnanto was furious and ran to tell Antonio who had to pay the maestro for the lesson and for a doctor to look at his cut head. That night, Lou got his ass kicked by his father, who then said, "Lou, if you think about it, we all learned today. You do not have the disposition to become a musician. Let's agree on no more music lessons," and then hugged his boy. Whenever Lou heard Antonio tell this story, he argued that Dr. Remnanto provoked him by calling him a talentless piece of shit. Still, whatever the case, Lou took up other hobbies, such as fishing, as opposed to playing guitar.

Antonio, as Walt described him, had white curly hair, a white handlebar mustache, a round belly, and always had a kind word for everyone. Walt rarely saw him angry, and Walt would go to his Grandpa when Lou was cross at him. When Walt came home from leave during World War II, Antonio demanded that he, not Lou, would prepare the Italian meal that Walt so desired. Walt said that his plate of al dente spaghetti was overflowing with sausages, meatballs, and braciole. Walt would devour three plates full while everyone else could barely tackle one plate of Grandpa's secret spaghetti sauce and pasta. Grandpa and Grandma loved to see Walt eat up and smile. "He will grow up to be a fine young man and make us proud," they would say with pride.

Walt told us that Antonio died just after World War II, and he said that he was the glue that kept the various aunts, uncles, and cousins together. When he passed away in 1947, Walt felt that after the funeral, many of his relatives would not be seen or heard from again. Unfortunately, Walt was correct with this prediction and said that some of his family died with Grandpa that sad day. Antonio was 74 when he departed but would have been very happy to see a large gathering of relatives, especially children, attending the funeral and wake.

Walt's Grandpa, Antonio, was truly a character, and this led to my investigating more about my mother June's father and mother. The story, similar to May's, started sad, but at least ended on a happy note.

Chapter 3

A Premonition at Lake Copake

W alt's father, Lou, was a driver for the Superintendent of the New York City Post Office. He was proud of his job and had two fringe benefits. One being that he got to drive around important public figures who were generally well connected in the New York Democratic Party. These officials got Walt his appointments to the US Military Academies (which Walt did not accept). The other being that he also had use of a car when he was not needed to drive the Superintendent.

In the 1930s, during the Great Depression, a car was a symbol of freedom; it was a privilege to actually leave the dirty, polluted, crime-ridden city for the suburbs and even the countryside. Walt's favourite memory as a boy was driving with his father and mother to a town roughly two hours north of the city called Copake. On Lake Copake, Walt's parents would rent a cottage only 100 feet from the lake. There, Walt would go fishing, hiking, boating, and hunting. With his father's shiny black Dodge, all the other children from New York were jealous of Walt's father and secretly wished their fathers worked for the government and had special privileges just like Walt's father, Lou.

Walt remembered that, one day, his father had to go back to the city for work and left Walt and his mother at the cottage. He knew everybody in the small, tight-knit community of roughly ten uniform, side by side, one-bedroom, living room, kitchen, and bath cottages. They were painted bright green and had screen doors and windows to keep out the bugs. Even in the summer, the cottages had a breeze from the large lake, and Walt usually slept with a light blanket.

One morning, his mother, May, said, "Walt, walk with me to the local boat camp and general store, as your father will be returning later this afternoon, and I need to buy some food for supper." Walt enjoyed walking with his mother and liked going to the general store. Maybe he would meet some other children? Perhaps even a girl his age? Certainly, he could convince his mom to buy him some taffy or a bar of Hershey chocolate. They walked to the store, which was about 1/2 mile away along a dirt path, and this was uneventful. The store visit was also mundane, other than Walt getting his mother to buy him two candies instead of one. Walt thought this was good, as Dad would only splurge for one or the other. Mom was a soft touch, and Walt knew this.

Strolling back to the cottage, they saw three men walking toward them. May recognized them from the cottages as they were unpacking their car yesterday. The men's ages ranged from their late twenties to early forties. As they approached May and Walt, they greeted them both and stopped for a chat. The men were Catholic priests, and they wanted to know where the general store was. After a short chat, the oldest man said "I am Father Boyle." He then introduced Father McKenna, who was roughly 35 years of age, and finally, he introduced Father Rory, a cheerful red-headed young priest still in his twenties.

As a bit of background, Lou was originally Catholic but converted to Lutheran to marry May, who was brought up in the German Lutheran Church. Neither May nor Lou was particularly religious, although, in keeping with the times, they went to Church at Easter, Christmas, and for any other reason like Holy Communion, Baptism, etc., but nothing more.

May introduced Walt and shook hands first with Father Boyle, then with Father McKenna. When May approached Father Rory, she knelt and took his hand and kissed his priest's ring. She said, "It is an honor to meet you, your Excellency." The Fathers and Walt were surprised about this and said that "Your Excellency" is for bishops and Father Rory is a newly ordained priest. With that, May said without hesitation, "Father Rory will become a bishop." Then she stood up and seemed to come out of a daze and apologized for talking nonsense. Everyone, a bit surprised, said goodbye, and went their separate ways. Walt was really embarrassed and said, "What was that about, Ma?" She said, "I don't know what became of me, but please do not tell your father what happened. He would not understand." Walt agreed to keep quiet.

That evening Lou returned from New York City and, during supper, asked if anything interesting happened while he was gone.

With that, there was a knock on the door and the three priests were standing there saying, "Hello, neighbors." Lou was polite, but in general, did not really trust clergy, as he was not religious and felt they were always looking for money. The priests then told Lou about what happened that day with May's comments to Father Rory, and they wanted to know more why she said such an amazing thing.

Lou's face lit up like a red lantern and curtly told the priests he was tired and asked them to leave. They were disappointed and noticed something was wrong and quickly left.

Walt never saw his father this angry before. "Are you crazy or what? They think you are a fucking witch. You will have everyone laughing at us. This is not normal. Don't you ever talk to them again and stop that fucking witchcraft... It is purely wrong. If you keep this up, you will be put in an insane asylum in chains. Cut it out. Now!"

May cried, and Walt tried to help his mother, but Lou said, "You will never get far if people think you are different. The world is harsh, and I could lose my fucking job because of your mother, and then we will live on the street." May continued to sob but assured Lou in between sobs that she would stop "this nonsense" and never let it happen again. The rest of the week was tense, but May did her best to make Lou forget his anger, and Walt worked overtime to be good and to keep the cottage tidy and to get Dad back to being frugal but nice. Lou got back into the holiday mood by taking Walt fishing and even took May to a Saturday night dance. There was peace again and Walt was happy.

Walt later said, "In the early 1950s, Father Rory became one of the youngest bishops in North America." May's prediction came true.

But another event, not paranormal but catastrophic, shaped Walt's view of the world regarding his love of flying and his memory of the awful event of May 6, 1937.

Chapter 4
Grandma's Ghost is My Co-Pilot

Walt told us about this encounter with the paranormal in his army service during World War II. He would always tell the story when, as a pilot, he had trouble with his PT-19 aircraft and the engine on this plane started to choke, sputter and stall at least 20 miles from the nearest airbase. He flew closer to the ground, as he knew that landing at a base was impossible, and he had to find a level strip of ground to land his plane to minimize serious injury to himself.

In the distance, outside of Montgomery, Alabama, he saw a farm with a straight dirt road and with no cars operating on it. He thought if he could get to this field, he could land on the road safely and also keep the now crippled aircraft in one piece. As the plane limped forward and continued its controlled yet rapid descent, a sight frightened him immensely. He saw from the cockpit high voltage wires crossing the field at roughly 50 to 60 feet above the ground. Walt knew that he was right on course to hit the wires and, in a flash, leave this Earth for hopefully a better place.

There was no room to maneuver, as his engine had now lost all power, and he was gliding toward the farm, the road, and the high voltage wires. Walt was petrified and started to wonder in this predicament if it would be better to dive the plane into the ground now or fly into the wires in roughly 10 seconds. He was right on course to hit the wires, and there was virtually no chance that he would miss either metal towers which held up the wires, or the wires themselves.

With only a couple of hundred yards to go at 75 miles an hour, Walt prepared for the worst. He started to say his prayers.

Suddenly he felt comforted by a warm light that chased the fear out of his system. He looked next to him at the empty instructor's seat in the cockpit and saw a flesh and blood image of his grandmother who died in 1937, more than six years previously. She was in her favorite dress; he smelt her gardenia perfume, and she smiled and nodded at him. He spoke with her by thinking, as he did not have to open his mouth, "Are you here to take me away?" Grandma answered, again in his head, "No, you will be fine." Walt looked forward and saw the impact would be in about three seconds. Grandma slowly faded away, but she maintained her warm and comforting smile as she disappeared.

The plane then had a sudden and gentle lift as a gust of wind ever so slightly stopped the rate of decline and actually raised the plane a few feet. At the time of impact, Walt felt the rubber tires bounce off the wires, and the plane shuttered but kept moving forward and now proceeded toward the dirt road. Walt wondered if the tires were damaged and whether the plane would summersault upon impact with the road. However, the plane touched down gently onto the dirt road, and Walt was able to hold the plane steady until it slowed to a complete stop.

While overcome with joy at his new lease with life, he had an overwhelming sense of peace and again smelt the strong smell of gardenia in the cockpit.

The investigators who examined the plane found that, due to faulty maintenance, the carbonator froze and Walt received a commendation for landing the plane without injuries to himself, others, or damage to his plane. At the age of 19, Walt tasted death for the first but not last time and felt it was a very bitter taste indeed.

He was always close to Grandma, who looked after him as a boy and kept him safe during the tough years of America's Great Depression. At the following Sunday service at the base, Walt asked the minister to say extra prayers of thanks to his Grandma, who helped co-pilot his flight to safety.

Walt's training was now promoting him from a new pilot to a more seasoned veteran. He was next transferred to Fort Myers, Florida, to train new pilots on how to fly B-17 bombers. While there, he unexpectedly came face to face with the enemy.

Chapter 5

Remember the Hindenburg Disaster, May 6, 1937

While Walt grew up in the midst of the Great Depression, he also remembered seeing great cruise ships docking in New York, including the RMS Queen Mary and the SS Normandie. He saw fast and great transcontinental trains and planes. A sight that he never forgot and talked about constantly was the visit of the LZ 129 Hindenburg in 1937.

In the 1930s, a fast ocean liner could take a passenger in luxury from New York to Europe in roughly five days. If they were going at flank speed, the trip tended to be a little rough as the ship allegedly vibrated as it was pushed to its limits. That is why passenger ships now take eight days to cross at a more comfortable pace. However, if you were important enough or rich enough to need to get to Europe faster than this, taking a Zeppelin could cut your travel time in half.

Walt remembered that the day the Hindenburg arrived and flew over New York, the school principal said the students could all go to the flat roof of the school to get a better look at this majestic airship. The students were excited and a school photographer went up and arranged to take photos of the airship as it circled the city before landing in Lakehurst, New Jersey.

The day started sunny but started to get overcast when they were told to go to the roof in an orderly fashion. Like a large prehistoric monster, the Hindenburg approached from Manhattan and started to circle over the Bronx. The children waved in excitement and they could see the passengers and crew waving as well. This craft was so large, so dominant in the sky but also quiet except the hum of the motors, which were not loud as Walt remembered.

The craft made another circle of the City as there were reports of thunder and lightning in New Jersey. The children were sad to see the craft lumber towards Lakehurst and all dreamed of the day they could enjoy the first-class travel of flying via Zeppelin.

Walt ran home to tell his mother and father what he saw, as he had never seen anything remotely like this. Yes, he had seen blimps, but they did not compare to the mammoth and elegant Hindenburg. Around supper time, Walt dominated the conversation telling his parents about the nuances he observed. All of a sudden, there was a loud rap on the door and their neighbor, Mr. Rudenstein yelled, "Turn on the radio; the Hindenburg just crashed!" At first, Lou said, "This must be a joke." However, May said, "Lou, turn on the radio."

Herb Morrison of CBS News described in detail what he saw and for Walt, Lou, and May, the description was a chilling yet descriptive account of the horror that took place on that day of May 6, 1937, when 36 passengers and crew were killed during the accident.

Walt was stunned and for the first time in his life, his father said, "Let's bow our heads and pray for both the victims and for the survivors." Walt prayed as hard as he could for the people he just saw a few hours earlier as the Hindenburg circled his school and waved to him and his classmates.

While the disaster dampened Walt's desire to fly in a Zeppelin or blimp, he maintained his love of fixed-wing air travel and enjoyed it both during the war and afterward as well.

While the Hindenburg disaster remained fixed in Walt's mind, he experienced a more personal and perhaps inwardly more transformational experience in the following year.

Chapter 6
Walt's Summer Adventure

Walt and his best friend, Raleigh, were just teenagers that summer in 1937. As they headed down Morris Avenue, they were looking for an adventure. In the dog days between summer break and fall classes, the enthusiasm of getting out of school was over and Walt was delighted to have been accepted into the Bronx High School of Science. The students there were more like his friend Raleigh and less like the under-aged thugs who tended to go to DeWitt Clinton High School. Walt's father hoped Walt would be inspired to become a doctor or a medical professional. This desire was less to do with serving the public and more to do with having a good-paying job in the 8th year of the Great Depression. However, the boys needed to do something that day, but they were not sure exactly what.

They wound their way down to a local playground, but the last thing Walt wanted to do is play baseball, as he was not very good with catching nor hitting, and it was still too early to convince anyone to play football. The search for something to do continued. But, they saw a group of young boys run up from an old, privately owned brownstone. Walt grabbed one boy and said, "What's wrong?" Out of breath, the boy said, "The police removed the body of Dr. Weiss from his house this morning. There is no one inside and the front window is open. "This is the opportunity we were looking for," said Raleigh. "He was an eccentric old man and had an interesting collection of weird and wonderful stuff." They looked at each other and knew something interesting was open to them if they dared to investigate.

Down the street loomed the dark, unkempt brownstone building owned by Dr. Weiss. The good doctor retired a good ten years ago from practising medicine in the neighborhood. As a doctor, he delivered Walt and Raleigh and was always there anytime day or night. After he retired, mothers and fathers still came to him for help, and at first, he reluctantly assisted. However, as his eyesight failed and his health went into decline, he more or less became a recluse except for his housekeeper, Aida, a lovely Portuguese woman, in her early forties who religiously came to look after him three times a week and cooked him meals and generally managed his accounts, as he became less able to help himself. Without Aida, Dr. Weiss was lost. However, even Aida couldn't help him when his heart finally gave up. Now the house was vacant, and a window in the back on the ground floor was partially opened. What should they do?

They concocted a plan. As everyone knew, Dr. Weiss was a bachelor and had no known relatives. "Let's search the house for something - guns, knives," said Walt. "Telescopes and microscopes," said Raleigh in reply. "You are strange, Raleigh. Who searches for microscopes and telescopes?" Walt asked. "Scientists," said Raleigh.

Raleigh was Walt's best friend. He was smart and came from a loving family. However, he suffered from polio and respiratory illnesses as a boy and needed to wear a clumsy brace on his leg. In the 1930s, he was subject to ridicule at school. Walt defended his friend with vigor and he joked this made Walt a better fighter. He took boxing lessons just to better defend Raleigh.

Together they sneaked to the rear of the garden where the window was partially open. The idea was that Walt would enter and then pull Raleigh inside. They had to be quick, as if a neighbor saw them entering, the cops would be called and they would be arrested. However, if, and only if, they could enter the building unseen, perhaps an Aladdin's Treasure would be open to them. All for the taking! They were scared, they were tempted, they were bored, and Walt entered the house. "What about ghosts?" "Well, hopefully it is too light for them to come out," Walt said but without conviction.

After pulling Raleigh into the house, they searched the living room. Old black and white photographs of long deceased ancestors of Dr. Weiss from Austria were lovingly hung on the wall. China cabinets were open and unknown objects were missing. They were not the first to enter the home, as there were signs of open desk drawers and most closets were open, and in some cases, clothing was lying disheveled on the foyer floor. Slowly decaying flowers smelt sickeningly sweet and somehow fit in as both Walt and Raleigh acknowledged that death had very recently visited this home. It felt as if Dr. Weiss would somehow materialize in front of them, or conversely, they would hear the tapping of his sturdy mahogany cane as he cautiously came down the stairs. After holding their collective breath for a moment, Raleigh got the courage to say, "Whatever we may be looking for is probably upstairs."

The boys ascended the wide wooden stairs; Walt first, now armed with one of Dr. Weiss's wooden canes - "Just in case." They looked around the dark and musty hallway. The carpet, probably Persian from at least a century ago, still looked relatively new, but everything else in the house looked worn, old, dusty, and again smelt of decay.

"Anything worth having is in his bedroom," Raleigh whispered as if each closed door had a mysterious and ghostly figure listening eagerly to the voices of the living. Walt said, "Let's go; I'm scared." Raleigh said, "Courage Walt; I will not leave you." The irony being Raleigh could move only slowly due to his disability. Walt felt somehow fortified by Raleigh's confidence. They tippy-toed to the last bedroom on the right-hand side, which apparently had an en suite bathroom. The room was, as expected, large, with old and fine linen and blankets on the large king-size bed. Again, evidence of earlier intruders was left as dresser drawers were open and clothing tossed carelessly on the floor. Raleigh opened a closet door, which led to a spacious closet, which was in itself the size of a small room.

Raleigh felt his heartbeat as he saw neatly laid out on a shelf a German Leica Camera and assorted lenses. "Wow, we hit the jackpot, Walt! What do you think?" Walt was amused at Raleigh's interest, as Walt felt Dr. Weiss must have a pistol, shotgun, or at least a sword hidden away. While Walt pushed the musty clothing aside, he did not find what he desired.

They left the closet open and decided to quickly check the other bedroom to see if there was anything else to claim for themselves. They entered the bedroom, which was made into a study by Dr. Weiss and found mostly leather-covered medical books in German, Latin, and English. Again there were many photographs obviously from the previous century, and to Raleigh's delight, a microscope dated from the early 1900s manufactured by C. Reichert of Wien. Raleigh squealed in delight.

However, the exuberance of the moment dissolved like sugar in hot tea when they heard slow and steady steps coming up the stairs. They were trapped! Walt, for a moment, looked at the second-floor window and calculated whether he could jump to a parallel branch of a sturdy oak, but looking at Raleigh, knew that he could never make the jump. Raleigh knew what Walt was thinking and said, "Go ahead, Walt; I will deal with whatever is coming up the stairs." Walt felt ashamed and said, "No, we will deal with it together."

A shadowy white figure appeared at the landing of the stairs. It was not much bigger than they were. Was it the ghost of Dr. Weiss coming for his just revenge, they wondered? The figure moved slowly but steadily toward them. Walt closed his eyes, as he never saw a ghost before and wondered if it would kill him. They could barricade themselves in a bedroom, but Walt figured the ghost would just go through the door and get to them anyway. Maybe they could dart past it but again Walt thought no; Raleigh is not agile.

The figure stopped and spoke, "What are you doing here? Don't you know the Doctor is dead? Don't you have respect for him?" The female foreign-sounding accent meant it was Aida, Dr. Weiss's housekeeper. She was crying, with a sorrowful plea to them to respect the dead and the life of the good doctor. While the boys were relieved that she wasn't a ghost, they were troubled by a spirit they did not know really existed. Aida was deeply hurt and was teaching them a lesson they could not learn in school and even not in church. She, by her unselfish devotion to Dr. Weiss and through the humanization of the pain she felt for the loss, taught the boys that being human was more than reading, writing, and going to school and church. It was loving others and respecting the lives of neighbors, both of those you know and those who are just acquaintances. They both felt shame.

Walt and Raleigh apologized to Aida and promised not to take anything. They also asked her if they could help her tidy up some of the mess made by other curious neighborhood children. She said, "No, I will look after the house, but you go home and do not come back. This place isn't for you." They said yes and exited through the front door instead of the rear window. As they got outside, the sunlight bothered their eyes. Walt saw some faded flowers in the dirt, bent down, and picked them up. They went back to the door and knocked, Aida quickly opened it and said, "What is it now?" in an angry tone. Walt and Raleigh gave the slightly wilting white flowers to Aida and said, "We are sorry for your loss." Aida fought off a smile, then turned her head to hide a tear. She appreciated the kind gesture.

Walt and Raleigh graduated from being little boys that day.

As Walt and Raleigh grew up and war clouds appeared on the horizon, Walt dreamed about being able to serve in the US Army Air Corps. Once World War II started for the US in December 1941, life changed, and Walt prepared to enter the service. In the meantime, Raleigh's health deteriorated, and sadly he passed away toward the end of the war. Walt never was able to properly say goodbye to his childhood friend.

However, Walt was soon excited to receive orders to report to Fort Dix, New Jersey, for basic training.

Chapter 7

"We Will Fight the Germans on the Beaches of Atlantic City"

One of Walt's first World War II army stories was when he was stationed at Fort Dix, New Jersey, for boot camp. One early autumn evening after training, all the recruits were told to muster on the parade ground. Once there, the Commanding Officer told them they would be transported in full uniform and with their non-working drill rifles to Atlantic City. No one knew why this instruction was given, but they were boarded onto transport trucks and driven approximately one hour to the beach. Once they arrived, Walt scanned the waterfront, which was familiar to him. His parents used to take him to Atlantic City as a boy, where he enjoyed the summer breezes on the cool boardwalk in the evening. The hotels were still there but used to billet troops, not for civilian tourists.

Then, thousands of troops were marched onto the sand of the beach and were told to stand at attention. As far as the eye could see, soldiers were doing so, spread out over the sands of Atlantic City. "Why are we here? Why are we doing this?" was whispered by the recruits while the drill sergeants told them to remain silent and to keep watch. "Watch for what?" The murmur amongst the now sagging troops was rising and the sergeants were having a harder time keeping the men quiet and focused on the blackness of the Atlantic Ocean without succumbing to the hypnotic sounds of the waves breaking on the seashore.

Finally, they were told why they were on the beach. There were claims of a German submarine, spotted by aerial reconnaissance, and to show the Germans the US was no pushover, there was a show of force on the beach. While the explanation was appreciated, it still left the recruits with a chilling thought. What if German commandos do land on the beach? Not one soldier or NCO (Non-Commissioned Officer) had bullets for their guns. In fact, a small raft of three or four Germans with submachine guns could take out the whole group. This fear was heard by the sergeants who instructed the recruits to "butt stroke" the Germans if they tried to land.

"Hmm, this does not seem like a well-thought-out plan," whispered Walt to his comrade next to him. The soldiers were getting cold, tired, and bored as they went from "attention" to "at ease." They even were told to march in place to stay warm and sharp. Walt was exhausted.

At dawn, they were told that the German submarine had retreated and that they could sit down in the sand. This was greatly appreciated, and then they received a second and even better surprise. At the large local hotels, hot breakfasts will be served and the recruits would be able to have bacon, powdered eggs, and creamed chipped beef on toast. This raised morale and at least the night wasn't lost in vain. Walt remembered that they saved America from the Axis, got to go to the beach, and had a delicious hot breakfast included. Not bad for a new recruit at Fort Dix in 1942!

Another incident happened while transferring to flight training at Beaver Falls, Pennsylvania. Walt was now entering advanced training and learning to fly a plane. However, discipline and training was still very tough and only marginally less rigorous than boot camp. As he traveled on a steam train that bellowed out thick smoke from the coal engines, he felt the sensation of getting warmer and his throat getting sore. The six-hour journey from New Jersey to Beaver Falls was unbearable in that he had to stand most of the way, and he felt the soot from the train's exhaust irritating his throat. Upon arrival, he hoped to catch a truck or bus from the station to the campus/barracks and get some needed rest.

However, after assembling in the parking lot, the Commanding Officer instructed the men to march uphill through the town of Beaver Falls, as the good citizens there wanted to cheer their troops on. Walt was in a bad situation, as he felt a fever coming on and his throat now could barely allow saliva to pass. He marched and marched, feet aching, back hurting and all of his joints were on fire. Perspiration was pouring from his head, and he was now dizzy, yet he marched.

Halfway up the hill, he started to stagger, but the drill sergeants refused to allow him to break ranks and ordered his two comrades next to him to hold him upright for the rest of the march but to keep going. At the top of the hill, Walt could barely stand and he was berated by his new sergeant, "You goldbricker! Go to the hospital, but if the doctors do not find anything wrong with you, you will be on KP (Kitchen Police) for two weeks after training and classes."

Walt stumbled to the hospital and was given a cot in a room with three other patients. He fell asleep and remembered waking up to have his throat painted with an antiseptic, which tasted horrible and felt worse when the solution touched his raw throat. He had a high fever and came in and out of consciousness. On the morning of the third day, a civilian nurse, who reminded him of his mother, gave him a glass of fresh orange juice. He drank the acidic drink and started coughing. She sweetly told him to sip, not gulp, and nurse it, as he needed to regain his strength.

Walt remembered this kind act of compassion, and as he drank the juice, he regained his strength and was soon able to rejoin his comrades in flight training.

Before long, however, Walt was transferred to Maxwell Field, Alabama, where he met one of his first nemesis, Colonel Lawrence Reeves. While there, he learned some valuable life lessons in friendship and faced down death with the help of an unexpected but helpful co-pilot later in his stay in Maxwell Field.

Chapter 8

A Race Against the Commanding Officer

Back at Maxwell Field, Walt had other experiences with the controversial Colonel Lawrence Reeves. He told these examples, which give more color and clarity to who his commanding officer really was, and what it was like serving under him.

When Walt first arrived at Maxwell Field, the air cadets had to fall into attention to hear from their new commanding officer and what they heard chilled them even on this hot summer's day.

Colonel Reeves started in his thick southern accent and said, "Welcome to Maxwell Field; I am your Commanding Officer - that's God to you," while he described himself as a moderate and humble man. He warned the cadets that there might be thieves amongst them but told them not to call the MPs or sergeants should they find any. He told them that they all had the authority to deal with it. He spat this out at the men as if he had shit in his mouth, "If you catch a thief, kill him." He added that no cadet would be in any trouble, as thieves are the lowest forms of scum on earth and his offices and non-commissioned officers were instructed to clear any man who kills one, no questions asked. Despite the less than comforting welcome, Walt did not hear of anyone missing money or personal belongings while in Maxwell Field.

Reeves used to talk endlessly to the men about how he was a champion runner when he was at Auburn University. While his university days were long behind him, he would wager that he could beat any cadet on a one-mile run. He goaded the men constantly in his tirades about discipline, character, and order. As pressure built on Colonel Reeves during the ongoing food complaints, when cadets routinely wrote home to complain about poor food and poor hygiene at the canteen, Reeve's rants and boosting escalated. This came to a climax one Sunday morning after chapel services.

In his weekly view of the world to his captive audience, Colonel Reeves accused the men of malicious rumor-mongering. He went on to say that not one man had the courage or conviction to take him up on his offer to race him for one mile, which would be fairly judged by Lt. Colonel "Bubba" Williams - "a fat-assed professional ass-kisser," the men joked behind his back. "You're all afraid! Would there be one man amongst you that had the courage in his convictions?" Reeves spewed out like a damaged sewer line polluting a pristine lake. He then said that if anyone took up his challenge and won the race, they could get a 10-day pass to go home. Walt, coming from New York, could not resist a challenge and thought that, after boot camp and advanced training, he was in the best shape he had ever been. Besides, Walt thought, "The food here sucks and I want to go home and have Mom's home-cooked meals." Walt stepped forward and said, "Sir, I accept your challenge." This in front of roughly 600 men and a dozen officers. Reeves and Bubba smiled with an evil grin and said, "Let's meet at 7:30 am tomorrow." All physical training was canceled for the day so that the men could see this cadet "get licked," grinned the 40-year-old Colonel. The men cheered more because tomorrow's PT was canceled than for supporting Walt, but money started to flow as bets were taken, and the odds were three to one against Walt.

Walt looked forward to the challenge and enjoyed the respect and the best wishes his comrades offered him. His drill instructor, Sergeant Dave Mingo, a young go-get-em Physical Training instructor from San Diego, asked him if he knew the Philosophy of Running. Walt said, "Win?" Mingo laughed and said "Yes, but let Reeves take the lead and set the pace. It will be four laps around the quarter-mile track. Stay within ten paces of him until the last quarter of the last lap and then run as if your life depended on it!" Sergeant Mingo wished him luck but said, "Officially, I need to root for that shit-ass Colonel." Walt was surprised, as officers made their way to his barracks that day or arranged to bump into him on the post and whispered, "Please beat that fucker." Walt wasn't fully sure how much Reeves was despised until that evening.

Walt got up and forwent any breakfast except for a slice of toast and a half glass of orange juice at 6 am and stretched and waited for the appointment. At 7:15 am, Walt got to the track where he was cheered-up by the sight of hundreds of NCOs and cadets circling the field to get a good view of the race. Colonel Reeves was as cocky as ever and said, "Where is my victim? Oh, I mean, my opponent?" Walt said, "Sir, I am here, Sir, and ready to begin." Reeves said, "Sit your sorry ass down, as I said we start at 7:30 and I mean 7:30, not 7:29 and not 7:31, you understand, boy?" Walt said, "Sir, yes, Sir," but he sensed for the first time that Reeves looked slightly bothered, or was it fear he sensed?

The lard-assed Lt. Colonel "Bubba" Williams instructed the men to shake hands, get on the mark, get set and GO! This happened at exactly 7:30 am, and there were no empty spaces between viewers all around the quarter-mile track. Colonel Reeves took off, like his house was on fire, Walt thought, and Walt had a tough time trying to keep roughly ten paces behind him. He never thought an old man of 40 years old would have this speed and stamina. Walt was not yet twenty and he felt embarrassed about how hard it was to keep ten paces behind. Walt soon slipped to 15 paces behind Reeves by the end of the first lap.

The second and third laps were almost the same as the first lap. Walt Struggled to keep 15 paces behind Reeves, yet he remembered what Sergeant Mingo said and, through maximum effort, closed the gap to roughly ten paces. As they finished the first half of the last lap, Walt sensed Reeves was slowing but ever so slightly; or perhaps Walt was getting his second wind, but for the first time he thought this might just be possible. He heard the crowd cheering him on and felt their best wishes. He did not want to disappoint them, but he also disliked Reeves - no, he hated him, and that is what drove him forward.

At the last 100 yards before the finish line, Walt felt like he just started to race. He went from a steady pace to a sprint. He felt the warm, humid breeze as he gained on Reeves. Reeves turned to look, as he felt or heard Walt breathing down his neck. While he managed for a second or two to increase speed, he could not hold the sprint, as he was exhausted, and with 10 yards to go to the finish line, Walt passed Reeves. He saw Sergeant Mingo and some of the officers overtly cheering for him.

Walt passed the finish line as he felt he was getting faster, while Reeves was too tired even to comprehend what just happened. All 600 plus in the crowd spontaneously cheered. Walt had beaten Colonel Reeves and the taste of victory was sweet, at least for the first few minutes. The officers and NCOs came by to congratulate Walt except for Bubba Williams, who ministered to Colonel Reeves. Reeves looked dejected, which elevated Walt's spirits all the more. This was a day to remember.

While Reeves had his hands on his knees trying to gasp in oxygen, Lt. Colonel "Bubba" Williams started backtracking on the 10-day pass, saying that the pass was not guaranteed; it was just a thought or suggestion. Sergeant Mingo protested vigorously on behalf of Walt and questioned the "Southern Chivalry," which Reeves vomited at many of his indoctrinations. In the end, Reeves agreed to three days, not ten. He muttered that he wasn't feeling well the day of the race but still wanted to set an example of racing against the odds. Everyone, including the officers, called this "chicken shit," and behind his back, Reeves took on the nickname "Lying Larry." Walt got into trouble from time to time with both Reeves and Bubba Williams but usually got bailed out by the officers and NCOs.

Walt was happy with his three-day pass as he had just met a girl in Montgomery and was able to finagle a long weekend with her. Walt got a few digs from some of the men who lost money betting against him, but overwhelmingly he won the support of the men at Maxwell Field during his stay at air training. Walt and Sargeant Mingo maintained a friendship that spanned the years and Mingo was Best Man at Walt's wedding seven years later.

While winning the race against Colonel Reeves was a highlight of his stay at Maxwell Field, Walt had an even more memorable experience about always being prepared for the ... worst! This time at Christmas.

Chapter 9

Always Be Ready!

At the US Army Air Corps base, Maxwell Field, Alabama, Walt was looking forward to his first Christmas away from home. Being the only child to two second-generation parents whose family name for the father and maiden name for the mother would sit proudly as representatives of two of the three major Axis powers, Walt often mused on this irony. However, he was a spoiled child. So spoiled that he turned down politically-generated appointments to West Point, Kings Point, and Annapolis for the US Army, Merchant Marine, and Naval Academies, as he wanted to join World War II and be a fighter pilot, not an academic, and he worried, "The war may end before my combat test becomes a reality." Walt's mother always doted on him and he knew a good thing when he saw it. Despite the Great Depression leading up to the war and his father's modest income as a US postal worker, Walt wanted for little and was able to manipulate his parents, especially his mother, as a rule. He was homesick and it hurt.

While grateful that the brutal Alabama sun was kinder and gentler in the winter, training was tough and army food routinely served was S.O.S. (Shit On a Shingle). What was this? Well, it was creamed chipped beef on toast. Once a week, it was almost acceptable, but served with overcooked vegetables three times a day, it made it almost inedible. Being too far from Montgomery to walk and spending most of his spare cash buying hamburgers and ice-cold Coca-Cola at the base's PX (Post Exchange), Walt joined the other enlisted men in complaining about the food, but to no avail.

It was rumored that Colonel Lawrence Reeves, was diverting much of the best meat to the local black market and for his personal gain, but saying this out loud would only get a soldier to march in full dress uniform from morning until the evening until he dropped exhausted.

Some wrote home and begged their parents to ask their congressmen to help. Even the well-known investigative reporter, Walter Winchell, the famous newspaper columnist, and friend of the regular soldier, was informed about the low morale and food issue at Maxwell Field. If an army marches on its stomach, then the troops at Maxwell Field were in the latrine with diarrhea. But despite rumors of investigations and congressional visits, nothing changed. Until Christmas Day.

Rather than having Reveille at 6 am, they were allowed to sleep until 8 am - an unheard-of luxury. Breakfast was pancakes, ham, and eggs. "Take what you want but eat what you take," was shouted out by the mess sergeant. Also, they were told to save room for Christmas dinner starting at 12 noon. It will be a feast!

Walt thought he died and went to heaven, and he got even more excited when he heard rumors that Christmas dinner would be Long Island duck, mashed potatoes, candied yams, orange sauce, and cornbread. After a filling breakfast, he ran to the PX, where he waited patiently to use one of the payphones to call his parents to tell them the good news. On the phone, his mother was delighted to hear from her son and happy that he was happy for the first time in six months. His father was happy too but warned, "Be careful; this doesn't seem right." As a US government employee, he knew senior civil servants, and presumably senior US Army officers could be vindictive if pushed. Walt said, "Don't worry, Dad; I'll be fine," and he hung up a little happier now that he spoke with his parents.

At 1 pm, despite the filling breakfast, everything he heard about the upcoming meal was true, except more! They were also served hot apple pie and vanilla ice-cream. Anyone who could eat more was welcomed to have a second roasted duck. Walt was tempted by the thought of seconds but knew he could barely finish what was in front of him, as the servings were huge. He got up after dinner and had to open his belt, as the combination of roasted duck in the afternoon and ham, eggs, and pancakes in the morning made him feel ready to burst. What he needed was a nap and later that evening planned to see the newest Hollywood film in the auditorium. This was looking at being the best day ever since joining the army!

Just as Walt returned to his barracks, he fell heavily on his cot and started to doze off, and then the world turned upside down. There was a commotion of bugles and the first sergeants yelling that all men must come to attention and prepare to march in full gear, which meant a backpack and M1 rifle. The men, still half-awake and groaning after eating the magnificent feast, were shocked to hear that they were ordered to march a 10-mile circuit in full gear "double time," meaning to jog.

"This must be a hoax," he thought, but by the time they got out of the base, one soldier after another started to keel over sick. A combination of overeating and perhaps a touch of food poisoning reduced the platoons to half size as the young soldiers keeled over in abdominal pain, vomiting, diarrhea, and hot with fever. Walt remembered the ham did not taste all that good and left most of it on the plate but ate everything else. Halfway through the forced march, the soldiers had a quick water break and had to double back and help assist, carry or pull sick soldiers who were lying next to the road. Walt thought, "I want to puke, shit, piss, bleed and cry." He never thought he would make it back, yet he and another able-bodied soldier had to help a sick comrade return to the base in "double-time."

Once he got back, he had to fall into a line to use the latrine as soldiers were still falling like flies. A few minutes later, there was another bugle call that signaled the remaining, able-bodied men had to assemble. There, Colonel Reeves, with his beady eyes and small stature hissed with his gritty Alabamian accent, "Y'all weak, y'all not ready, y'all must always be ready." He then went on to say that every man that dropped out of the forced march due to illness had to complete it as soon as possible, within 24 hours AND they needed to march in full dress uniform for 12 hours before they could take any future leave.

The film that evening was canceled due to low turnout, and rumor had it that the cooks knew or were told the ham was a little off or tainted.

As for Colonel Reeves, he was relieved of his command and reassigned to the Pacific. Officially, he died heroically in Okinawa. Other rumors went around, though, suggesting that he did die on Okinawa but not because of enemy action!

Walt never forgot his first Christmas away from home and in the army.

Chapter 10

June's Parents, Harry and Maise, in the Early 20th Century

Walt's father, Lou, and mother, May, were not the only sources of information about the past; June's mother, Maise, and her father, Harry, also had a story to tell. When they were about 80 years old, one evening, before watching the 1976 All-Star baseball game at their home, they started talking about the past. I remained quiet and listened, as I wanted to know their history. This is what they said.

Harry's father, Frederick, emigrated from Germany and settled in Queens, New York. Before coming to America, he served as an officer in the Franco-Prussian War at the rank of captain. Grandad showed me a French bayonet Frederick picked up at a battlefield during this brief but bloody war. The weapon was displayed in the foyer of his small two-bedroom, two-bath home in a West Florida retirement community. Harry was proud of the article and it was one of the only things he owned that once belonged to his father.

Frederick was a businessman and opened a type of microbrewery using the old German method of brewing beer, like in the Fatherland. He was a devoted Luthern and believed in hard work and tough discipline. Harry worked in his father's small company and told me that shortly after he was born in 1896, his father was listed in Queen's County "Who's Who" as an outstanding member of the community. Harry did not particularly enjoy working at the brewery and didn't really like beer either. He would rather have attended school but also found it boring except for mathematics. His father passed away just prior to World War I, and apparently, there was little, if any, inheritance for him. Harry went to work at US Rubber Corporation and stayed with the firm until he retired as Treasurer in the early 1960s. He made a comfortable living, but by no means was it excessive.

Harry had a passion for baseball and would take any and all opportunities to play, or better, watch, America's favorite pastime. He enjoyed watching the Brooklyn Dodgers and New York Giants, and he would travel to Upper Manhattan to see the New York Highlanders, who became in 1911 the New York Yankees. By chance, he found accommodations in the Bronx and became an avid Yankee fan in particular, but still supported all the New York teams in general, a rarity even in those days, but as Harry said, "I love baseball almost as much as Maise." He would then get a loving slap from Maise, and then I heard her story, which was a little bit tragic.

Maise was born in 1896 of Irish parents and lived near but not in Five Points, Manhattan. This area was notorious for poverty and crime, particularly amongst the Irish immigrants in New York City.

Her father owned a saloon not far from Tammany Hall and, from what she remembered, life was good until she was almost six years old. Maise's mother died soon after she was born and her father was busy running the saloon. It was her sisters who really brought her up during her father's absence.

With a tear in her eye, she said that just before her 7th birthday, for which her father had promised a new doll, he went to work early one morning. The saloon opened around 11 am where salt beef (corned beef) sandwiches were served for "free" with the purchase of a beer, which cost five cents. There is an old saying in America; there is no such thing as a free lunch as the patron had to buy a beer in order to eat the food.

Apparently, two men entered the saloon, causing trouble with the patrons. When Maise's father asked them to leave, one of them pulled out a gun and shot him in the chest and the face. He was taken to a nearby hospital and pronounced dead on arrival. The police had no leads on who killed him, and the case remains unsolved.

Maise remembered relatives of her father came, and her brothers and sisters were divided and sent to live with different uncles and aunts. She was given a home reluctantly by her father's older brother, who was a New York City police captain. He, however, already had a large family and a whole gang of children. Maise went from being Daddy's Princess to a servant to the police captain and his wife. As he was a mounted policeman, his boots were muddy and full of clinging horse manure. She needed to have them spit-polished every day before he went to work. She had to keep his uniform spotless and do laundry and cleaning. Maise was allowed to go to school, but only if she finished her work. She remembered how she was beaten severely by her aunt if her chores were not completed, and she was made to feel that she could be thrown into the street if she misbehaved, complained or did not express enough gratitude.

Maise and Harry met at a mixed dance during World War I; it was usually not appropriate for Irish and Germans to socialize. They had something in common - tough childhoods, a passion for baseball, and a need to find their own way in this unforgiving metropolis that was New York City. They dated only six months and were head over heels in love. Harry's parents were dead, and Maise's guardians objected to Harry but would agree to a marriage if he converted to Catholicism, which he did wholeheartedly. He loved Maise and would do anything for her, including changing his religion. Their favorite song was "A Bicycle Built for Two," and they would insert their own private words, which had special meaning to them and would giggle when singing the song even in their 80s.

Maise recalled she was pregnant with her first child, Harold, in 1919 - June's older brother. While World War I just ended, the world was now plagued with the Spanish Flu. She was in her early twenties, and as she was having a difficult pregnancy, her doctor recommended that she be admitted to a nearby hospital where they would be ready for all contingencies. Maise was clever enough to reject the idea, as she said that, in 1919, people checked into hospitals but were later carried out via an undertaker. She felt hospitals were not a safe place during an epidemic and stubbornly resisted all efforts for her to be admitted.

Harold was born at home with the help of a midwife, and there were no problems with the delivery. However, she endeavoured to keep most people away from her, except, of course, her husband, and took her baby to the roof of her tenement building for clean air and sunshine. She heard many friends and acquaintances fell ill and sometimes died of the Spanish Flu. However, Maise and baby Harold, along with her husband, survived the epidemic, and in fact, Harold lived to a ripe age of 92 years old.

I enjoyed actively listening to their stories and watched their eyes meet as they spoke. Their lives financially and socially got better after marriage, and they had three children, including my mother, June.

What sticks to me to this very day is what they said to me that evening. "We have had hard times and arguments but, if anything, we love one another even more than when we first met over 60 years ago." Do I believe this? Yes, for sure, as I saw it in their eyes and how they tenderly held one another's hands when they told me their stories. I still think of them often.

Harry and Maise both passed away a few months apart in 1979 and are buried together.

When Walt was in a rare good mood in the 1970s, we were able to probe him and his mother to extract memorable recollections about their lives during the Great Depression. Both May and Walt told the following story separately. It mostly matched up, but Walt's recollections seemed more vivid and descriptive than his mother's.

Chapter 11

Walt Versus Germany in the Gulf of Mexico

Walt's only other combat situation in World War II was once again Walt versus a German U-boat, and that was in the Gulf of Mexico when he was stationed near Fort Myers, Florida. Walt told the story that he was training pilots how to fly B-17 bombers and, while doing this, petitioned his commanding officer to allow him to join the war either in Europe or in the Pacific. He fancied living in the countryside in "Merry Olde England" and heard the pubs served warm beer, and the English girls were even warmer toward American airmen. However, all Walt's petitions to transfer were either postponed or declined.

Meanwhile, German U-boats were having a field day sinking freighters and oil tankers in the Gulf of Mexico. Walt said if you went to one of the usually pristine white sand beaches of West Florida, it was always covered with blobs of oil from sunken oil tankers. One day, Walt got a call to report to his B-17 for a combat mission.

It was early 1944 and reconnaissance aircraft spotted a U-boat around 120 miles North West of Fort Myers in the Gulf. Walt's aircraft was being loaded with depth charges as he got the coordinates of the last sighting of the U-boat. Weather was good and his crew was eager to engage the enemy.

They took off and sped to the coordinates to begin a zig-zag search for the U-boat. All eyes were peeled as they crossed miles of empty sea, and the only things they did spot were occasional friendly merchant ships or fishing vessels. They got a little antsy as the co-pilot suggested that they activate the depth charges and drop them anyway, as at least it would give them something to do! Walt disagreed, as he wanted to engage the enemy at least once in this "damn war which was passing us by."

As they were starting to consider going back, as the fuel in the tanks was under 50 percent, they saw a long dark object in the water. "Shit, I think I see it!" Walt shouted, and they flew a tight circle around the object to keep it in sight.

The bombardier checked his charts to make sure no American or Allied submarines were in the area, but there were none for at least 200 miles. This must be the German sub!

The crew armed the eight depth charges and swung long, low and slow above the calm Gulf of Mexico. The bombardier took control and gave Walt instructions on how to approach the target. About 500 yards before they reached it, they released their payload. The eight depth charges hit the water with a large splash and then, as they were timed, exploded, sending a plumb of water and smoke into the clear blue sky. "Did we get it?" Walt asked as they made a hard right turn and banked the large plane to circle back to the target area.

What they saw was oil floating to the surface and slowly, the dark submarine faded out of view as it sank deeper into the water. "We got it. A confirmed kill." The men celebrated and they promised one another that they would take turns to buy the beer once they returned to Fort Myers.

Walt felt vindicated that he didn't release the depth charges too early, and the thought that he sunk a U-boat may work in his favor for a combat assignment. Upon return to the base, Walt and the crew debriefed the intelligence officers. They felt proud to do their part in the war effort.

However, Colonel Andrew De Wolfe, a forty-five-year-old up and coming commanding officer who worked his way through the ranks without the usual political backing, wanted to have a quiet word with Walt. Walt was asked to tell the Colonel what happened and he listened politely without interruption. De Wolfe then said, did you ever think the U-boat may have released oil and submerged to avoid a follow-up attack? Walt was caught off guard. He was lost for words, but Colonel De Wolfe kindly said, "Let's call this a "probable kill" but not an "actual kill", as I would rather have more evidence than an oil slick and two or three photos of oil. Good job and congratulations to your men," De Wolfe said, "but next time, get more evidence. Details matter," he said with a broad smile.

Walt appreciated what the colonel said and also agreed, at least in his heart, that he was right about a potential fake oil slick. However, for a few weeks, there were no U-boat attacks in the area and Walt and his men did have a celebration, did get somewhat drunk on low alcohol beer, and this was the only example of Walt in a combat situation during World War II.

After the war ended in September 1945, Walt looked forward to being mustered out of the military and waited patiently for his honorable discharge. In 1946, he was sent back to Fort Dix, New Jersey to formally leave the military. While he wouldn't miss the rigid discipline, he did think he would miss flying and vowed to fly privately. He did so to the detriment of Uncle Auggie, and Walt told this following story over and over again with relish.

Chapter 12

Walt and Uncle Auggie's Big Adventure

Uncle Auggi was Walt's uncle, husband to Aunt LouLou, who was his mother's sister. Auggie was a strong-willed Scandanavian, who was a perfectionist when it came to carpentry. He did everything meticulously and if something was worth doing, it was worth doing right. There was a family legend that just after World War I, Auggie liked to go fishing in New York Harbor. He and his brothers would beach their rowboat on a small deserted island that was used by other fishermen, and later rum runners during prohibition. The thing is, Auggie could not leave things alone and always had to "improve" things whenever he could. Finding bricks, wood, and some abandoned tools on the island, Auggie became less interested in fishing and more interested in building a small cabin to keep him and other fishermen warm. As he did not have nails, he joined the wood without the use of steel nails. Throughout a long summer, Auggie, with a little help from his brothers and friends, built a fishing cottage and fireplace that could withstand the elements of the ferocious New York winters.

However, when the harbor patrol and Coast Guard found the island to be a perfect place for bootleggers, they "nationalized" the island and prohibited unauthorized landings, which meant this applied to Auggie and the fishermen who enjoyed fishing as a break from their hard manual labor five to six days a week. "The Government claimed the island and stole my cottage," laughed Auggie, as he was proud that rather than tearing down his cottage, the Coast Guards made it an office for a permanent representative. He felt honored in a way and enjoyed telling this story.

Uncle Auggie was a bit of an odd fellow. He was drafted into the army in World War I and was sent to France and fought on the front line. He told the family the stories of rats everywhere and maggots infesting everything. He was almost blasé about this, but the one thing he couldn't let go was when the Germans bombarded their lines. One day, Auggie was caught out of his shelter and a shell exploded nearby. He was wounded, and whilst he recovered from the shrapnel, he unfortunately lost most of his hearing. Back then, everyone said, "Auggie is hard of hearing," but even with a hearing aid the size of another ear, he couldn't hear much at all. You had to shout at him and speak clearly as he learned to read lips. He also spoke loudly, which scared Roots and me when we visited him as children, but we were told that was because he was hard of hearing and not angry at us. Actually, he was pretty fucking deaf, but no one wanted to admit this, especially not Auggie.

Now Walt heard the story about the cottage and how Auggie lost his hearing at least 100 times if he heard it once. Walt could not understand how Auggie would spend his holidays working; Walt was not put together like that. Walt's father, Lou, once said, "Walt always looked for the very least he could do to help a family member in a non-emergency." Lou laughed, but deep down, this must have grated a little. Walt pretended not to notice the barb.

Walt's real passion was airplanes. Even after being discharged from the US Army Air Corps in 1946, Walt continued to fly private planes as a hobby. Flying an airplane was the closest you could get to "dreaming while you are awake." He would often spend one weekend a month in Westchester County flying at a private airfield. Most of his spending money was used here and on the newest cars coming back into the market after the war.

One day, Walt visited Aunt LouLou and Uncle Auggie and a thought occurred to him. "I can kill two birds with one stone. I can take Uncle Auggie up for an airplane ride and some doctors believe a rapid change in air pressure could reverse or at least somehow mitigate deafness." The win-win here was Walt could get Auggie to pay for the rental hours of the plane, which was an expense of 50 dollars an hour in 1946, fuel included. Walt explained this to Auggie and Auggie was not amused. He quoted the famous saying, "If God wanted man to fly, he would have given him wings." However, Walt and Aunt LouLou said, "Auggie, get your stubborn backside into the plane, or never complain again about your hearing problem." Auggie liked to complain, so he reluctantly agreed to go with Walt to an airstrip near Croton Dam and take an hour flight in the hopes of curing or at least improving his hearing.

Auggie was roughly 50 years old at the time and was a tall, six feet, thin, and mostly bald man with thick glasses and a huge hearing aid. Walt told him to fasten his seat belt and together, in a small Cessna, they took off and climbed into the bright autumn sky. Walt took the Cessna up to just under 10,000 feet and dove it to 5,000 and climbed again and dove again. As Auggie was never in a plane before, he looked to Walt as being white as a ghost. Auggie was silent and Walt kept yelling, "Can you hear anything yet?" Auggie said, "No, let's go home." Walt was not about to turn back only 20 minutes in a 60-minute flight but gave up on the altitude changes and decided to give Auggie a tour of Croton Dam from above. Auggie was not impressed, but Walt was just happy to be flying.

As Walt banked the plane to start the homeward leg of the journey, they both felt a shutter as the plane lurched like a bucking bronco. "Shit, what the fuck is this?" Walt thought. Auggie was staring at him with both fear and anger. Walt then heard the engine sputter. He tried adjusting the carburetor, but this didn't help. They had fuel, but it was having a hard time getting into the engine. The motor sputtered more as Walt leveled the plane, looked at his map, and saw he was 12 miles from the airstrip, and if he had to glide at 5,500 feet altitude, he could only go two miles at best. With that, the engine stopped completely and Walt and Auggie were in the silent plane over the Croton reservoir. Walt radioed the tower and told them of his predicament, and they radioed back and told him to ditch in the lake. As the weather was clear and summer just came to an end, the lake was smooth and the water temperature was still relatively warm. "We will send out a boat to collect you both, happy landing."

Auggie could not hear what the tower said and he was virtually going into shock. Walt yelled and signaled that they would land on the lake and it should be alright. Auggie became whiter, if this was possible, and violently shook his head back and forth. "I can't swim, you asshole!" Auggie said. "I will fucking drown." Walt knew that Auggie rarely cursed, so he must really mean he could not swim. Walt found this unusual, as Auggie used to go fishing in New York Harbor, but now was not the time to argue.

Unfortunately, Walt had no good options now. If he landed on the water and got injured during the crash landing, then it was likely they would both drown. Walt was a good swimmer, but he would have to land 100 feet from shore and this would be a big risk.

There were no roads he could get to, and tall pines - a virtual forest - surrounded lake Croton. There were no clear spaces to get to and time was running out, as he was down to 2,000 feet and falling rapidly, but at least in a controlled descent.

Walt banked the plane and got back over the shoreline. Walt decided to land on top of the trees. This, too, was a risk and a big one, as he would brush the top of the pines to try and come to a halt and see what happened next.

As they made their final descent and were 100 feet above ground, Walt tried to start the engine again, but no luck, a controlled crash landing was imminent. Walt told Auggie to brace for the crash, and they slid along the tops of densely packed pine trees as the plane shuttered, bounced but kept upright as it slowed from the impact speed of 65 miles an hour. Walt started to think, "We just may make this out alive," and then the plane abruptly stopped. Walt and Augie looked at each other and smiled.

Just then, the plane, ever so slowly, started to tilt forward and soon, Walt heard the cracking of dozens of small branches, which meant the 50 feet down may not go as smoothly as the rest of the descent. Finally, there was a big crack as the final branch gave way, and the plane tumbled toward the ground, but a few smaller branches helped slow their dive to Mother Earth on the way down. The plane hit the ground front first with the propeller smashing into the pine needle covered ground. Both men, despite the seat belts, received light head and upper body injuries. Auggie dislocated his shoulder and, in pain, pulled himself out the still working door, and said, "This is the last time I am going to fly with you!" and he meant it too.

A rescue team arrived in less than 15 minutes as Walt got Auggie away from the aircraft in case it exploded, but fortunately, it didn't. They were both checked out at a local hospital, and were both released that day. Walt found the day exhilarating and took his future wife, June, out for dinner that night.

Uncle Auggie did recover quickly and returned to fishing and various handicrafts but never felt the urge to visit relatives via airplane. In fact, he never took a plane again, nor did he ever want to explore exotic treatments for his loss of hearing. "My hearing loss is freedom from Aunt LouLou's nagging," he would say with a grin. He remained stubbornly bound to earth and would repeat to Aunt LouLou when she wanted to fly to Florida to visit relatives, "If God wanted man to fly, he would have given him wings." This was Auggie's subtle way of saying, "No!"

After the experience with Uncle Auggie, Walt put his name on the list to enter the New York City Police Department. The list was long, as former servicemen who were returning home were looking for a steady job but with a little excitement. Walt waited almost four years to be called up, and in the meantime, worked in the post office with his father. The money and hours were good. Enough to enjoy his hobbies and to go out with his fiancée, June. However, he found his existence at the post office criminally boring and couldn't wait to join the police and experience a more exciting life. The following story was one of his first experiences out of the Police Academy.

Chapter 13
A Cop Fighter

Life in the 50th Precinct was not always driving in police cars but also walking the beat. Walt told a story about how he came face to face with a "cop fighter" in an area near Van Cortlandt Park in the Bronx. As Walt was a rookie and only walking the beat for a few weeks in his brand new blue uniform, the incident was etched into his mind.

One evening, he was approached by two middle-aged men who said there was a disturbance at a bar just a block away and around the corner, where two men were fighting. At the time, Walt had to call in the incident on a police telephone landline and then quickly made his way to the bar. There were mostly men milling around outside. They told him that a youngish well-built man, with red hair, a light brown jacket, and denim trousers, was a little tipsy and started a fight at the jukebox inside the bar. He just left the scene a minute or two ago running toward the park.

Walt ran off in the direction the small gathering indicated and came across a building that was being renovated. He saw what looked like his suspect trying unsuccessfully to climb a chain-link fence. Walt came up to the suspect and grabbed him by the collar and told him he was under arrest. The suspect smelt of beer and was chuckling. Walt said, "We will go to the 50th Precinct, and you can dry up and later go home." However, the suspect said, "I got a better idea; let's you and I fight." He turned with agility and punched Walt with a great deal of force, which propelled him backward. Walt admittedly enjoyed the challenge and started to exchange punches with the man. One punch by this character knocked Walt clean off his feet, and the suspect said, "Officer, it is a shame you couldn't last a little longer in the ring; I enjoyed the fight," and took off.

Walt got up to pursue the man who had about a half-block lead. The tipsy man tripped and fell, and as he was getting up, Walt whacked him with his nightstick, and he fell down hard. The man pushed himself up, which surprised Walt in consideration of the hit he gave him, and the man said, "OK officer, let's continue the fight." He grabbed Walt in a bear hug and, with force, threw him onto the ground. He could have lunged or even kicked Walt in the head, but instead waited for Walt to get up and got into a boxing stance and tried to box with Walt.

Walt wasn't having any more nonsense and swung his nightstick and again connected with his head. The suspect bolted toward a row of houses. Walt caught up with him again and the guy swung and connected, which knocked Walt to the ground. "Officer, fight like a gentleman." He was not menacing but almost playful, very strong, stubborn, and drunk. For the third and final time, Walt swung his nightstick, which bounced off his head like a bat hitting a baseball. Although Walt drew blood, the suspect ran down the street, but was cut off by two veteran policemen from the 50th Precinct in a patrol car.

This, if anything, infuriated the man who now wanted to fight all three policemen. The two cops struggled with the suspect and Walt joined the fracas. In the end, they tackled the man and were able to get his hands into handcuffs, but not before he hit all of them again, and not before he took a few more hits by the veteran cops, who used not pine but cocobolo wood. This made their nightsticks as hard as iron, which eventually wore the man down.

The oldest cop, a 20-year veteran who knew all the ins and outs of the police department, said, "This guy, Thomas Monahan, is known all over the 50th Precinct. He is a good ole Irish construction worker, who always attends church and is the pillar of the community until he drinks; then he is not. We will put him in the drunk tank at the 50th until he sobers up, and then his wife can come and collect him."

"By the way," he added, "did you enjoy your fight? He never kicks, nor will he use a knife, but he feels the best fights are with cops and firemen." Walt admitted he did enjoy the fight but was feeling sore and needed to soak in a hot bath tonight.

The veteran cops said they would arrest him for breaking the peace and he would be fined. Anything else and he could lose his job. He had a lovely family with two boys and a girl he needed to look after. Walt shook his head and asked for a ride back to the 50th, as he had a headache after all of this evening's excitement.

A week later, Walt heard a familiar voice, "Officer, officer!" It was Thomas and he was well-spoken, polite, and sincere, when he apologized and thanked Walt and the other policemen for not pressing charges. He said, "I have been working overtime and needed to let off some steam. I promise to try to be good," he said with a smile and with his fingers crossed, and strolled down the street. Walt had a few more encounters with Thomas, but they were, fortunately, less violent.

For Walt, a more harrowing event occurred when he was assigned to guard the Chinese Consul's residence. There was no fighting nor gunplay, but there was an unusual break in, which Walt told us about when he was in good spirits and not feeling too cold.

Chapter 14

A Diplomatic Incident Narrowly Averted in the Bronx

Early in the winter of 1951, Walt was a young rookie police officer assigned to the - mostly posh - 50th Precinct. Back then, it was known as the Country Club Precinct, as the upper-class suburb of Riverdale, in the Bronx, mostly fell within the 50th Precinct's boundaries. This area was predominantly wealthy Jewish, with a pinch of working-class Irish and Italians. The area Walt worked in overlooked where the Hudson and Harlem Rivers merged. You could see the tip of Manhattan from the high position in the Bronx. The Henry Hudson Parkway built by Robert Moses wound its way up through Riverdale on to Westchester County. The area was considered then, as now, one of the safest areas in New York City to reside. Many of the foreign consulates in New York had residences in the area. In 1951, two years after fleeing Mainland China, the Embassy of the Republic of China, now known as Taiwan, had its consulate in the 50th Precinct.

Why was this memorable for Walt? He would tell you that it was here, on a bitterly cold February evening, that he almost froze to death. Sounds like a classic Walt story, and my brother and I wondered if he meant it, but after hearing the same story over and over again, yes this definitely happened. As a matter of fact, to save Walt's freezing ass, he almost started a diplomatic incident. Here is how it goes.

As a rookie, you get the shitty assignments and guarding a consulate is not only mind-numbingly boring but bad for your health. What happened is that Sergeant O'Malley dropped Walt in front of the Chinese Consulate's residence just after midnight one bitterly cold February night. The temperature plunged to under 20 Fahrenheit. Walt was told to stay in front of the consulate at all times except once an hour, when he had to walk around the building to make sure it was secure, with no signs of break-ins. Walt stood for an hour and first felt the cold travel up from the soles of his shoes through his legs into his lower back. He said, "The cold feels as if you are getting an ice-cold epidural and enema at the same time." Now Walt was in fine physical shape, and with his NYPD-issued overcoat and leather gloves, he, at first, did not see a problem, but boy, did it get cold outside. Walt found a bit of relief walking around the building. By the third hour, he felt he was losing sensation in his toes and fingers. He walked to a nearby police phone and asked if he could be relieved for 30 minutes to warm up and regain circulation in his feet and hands. Sergeant O'Malley barked, "You cocksucker; do your job, or you will be busted out of the police department. Do not abandon your post, as we have no other officers who can guard the consulate. Do we understand each other?"

Walt knew where he stood. Retreat was not an option and there would be no relief until 7:30 am - another four hours, and the temperature continued to drop. Walt was thinking, "How do I survive, and yet keep my job?" He increased his patrols around the consulate to keep his blood circulating and in the outside hope of attracting the attention of a Chinese guard or servant. He even resorted to picking up pebbles and throwing them at the windows of the residence in the hope of waking up a servant. However, the wind was howling, and Walt was getting colder and colder and felt he was freezing to death. No one was awake inside the building and he shivered and shook. The situation, he thought, was getting worse.

By 5:00 am, Walt knew he had to do something. Weighing the options, he decided to walk around the building again in the hope a cook would be up to make breakfast for the staff of the consulate. As he approached the kitchen, he saw nothing but darkness and he was shivering intensely. "It was time to act," he thought.

Walt took out his NYPD-issued nightstick and broke the glass above the servant's entrance door into the building. He reached in and unlocked the door without cutting himself. He half thought this would set off alarms, but if alarms were present, they were silent. He entered the kitchen, which was not heated but still much warmer than outside. He was protected from the wind, the cold, the snow and ice. He thought he would stay here until morning, and then figure out what to say to Sergeant O'Malley.

Just then, he heard two voices, one male and one female, as they entered the kitchen and turned on the light. Apparently, they were up to start preparing for breakfast and screeched in horror as they saw the half-frozen policeman in the kitchen entrance.

The scream alerted internal security, and now four guards were in the kitchen armed with pistols. A more official voice then sounded, and the guards and servants bowed as the Consul General came to the kitchen to find out what the racket was all about. The mature Chinese gentleman spoke English fluently and asked why Walt was inside the building. Not knowing what to say and assuming he would at least be fired and possibly jailed for breaking into a foreign consulate, Walt told him he was bitter cold and was looking for warmth. The diplomat instructed the servants to bring

Walt hot tea and warm congee, a type of rice porridge. Walt was temporarily saved.

At 7:30 am, Sergeant O'Malley came to collect Walt, but was met by the Consul General, who told him he was negligent for not building a shelter for his NYPD police guards outside the building, and that he instructed the officer to come into the building to stay warm. The Consul General did not mention the break-in by Walt.

O'Malley, a tough and streetwise cop, knew bullshit when he heard it. He looked around and pointed to the broken window, and was told by the Consul General that one of the clumsy servants broke the window. Sergeant O'Malley just shrugged and told Walt to get into the car.

On the ride back to the station house, O'Malley was uncharacteristically quiet until they arrived. He said he didn't want to cause a diplomatic incident, but he thinks Walt broke into the consulate. He said, "You must have a shamrock up your arse to protect you, but if the consul does not want to complain formally, I will not either."

Walt said he and his new wife, June, celebrated that evening with a hot Chinese meal in Riverdale. However, as much as possible, he tried to avoid consulate duty, especially in the winter. But he bought a pair of thermal underwear, just in case.

Chapter 15

Walt's First Murder Case, 1953

efore his move to the 24th Precinct, Walt was a rookie detective, just learning the ropes up in the 34th Precinct in North Manhattan. While not as posh as the 50th in Riverdale, the 34th had an eclectic mix of rich and poor, black and white, and for post World War II New York City, it was as good as anywhere in terms of being an average precinct and a representation of New York City in 1953.

He was excited about his new job as a detective and while solving burglaries and following up on armed robberies were "fun," he longed for a good case, one that he could cut his teeth on - a murder. One day he got his wish, but like most cases, it didn't resolve itself like he initially expected.

Walt was called to an apartment where a young woman was dead, with a bayonet through her heart. She was blond, voluptuous, and retained her beauty, even as the last of her lifeblood seeped out of the wound in her chest as she laid naked on the white sheets, which were now turning crimson along with the underlying mattress. Her eyes were closed and she seemed to radiate a sense of calm and beauty despite her deadly demise.

A patrolman on the scene said, "She could have been a pin-up girl on my locker door at the station." His partner added, "What a waste; she is gorgeous, even in death." Walt asked what happened. The senior policeman on the scene said, "Her husband said he was cleaning his bayonet on the side of the bed when she jumped on him from the shower unexpectedly, and accidentally the bayonet pierced her heart. She died within seconds, and he immediately called the police."

"This sounds like horseshit," said Walt, "Where is the husband?" " He is in the living room and we are going to take him to the 34th Precinct for questioning." At that time, Sergeant Timothy Skinner arrived. Being a 15-year veteran on the force, he possessed a unique blend of political awareness and support for the cops on the firing line. He said he would happily take the scumbag in for robust questioning should Walt want to assign the case to him. Walt saw the husband, sitting on a sofa with his arms crossed, looking upset, but noting that he did not necessarily seem sad about his wife's demise. He was suspicious and therefore keen to interrogate him himself and declined Skinner's offer. Walt tried an old cop trick, which works in the movies and on the radio, but rarely in the field, but what the heck, "Why did you do it?" The man looked up and said basically the same thing Walt heard from the patrolman earlier, "I was home from work, I took out my bayonet and was cleaning it, when my wife came out of the shower, and not knowing I had a sharp edge in my hand, jumped on me, as we like to do it rough, and I accidentally stabbed her." Walt said, "Sure," with total sarcasm, and ordered the husband to be arrested and brought to the station for questioning.

It was an open and shut case, as there was no mystery at all. The husband admitted to killing the woman by accident. If he gets a good lawyer, he could get off on second-degree murder in terms of having a lovers' spat, and in a moment of passion stabbing her. Yet, Walt also thought, "There was no passion or remorse by the husband, just some concern over the situation. Perhaps there was more to this than meets the eye?"

When Walt arrived at the station, he found that the husband, Stephen Park, was a highly decorated former Marine captain who served in the Pacific in World War II and in the Korean War. "This guy is an all-American hero," said Skinner and jokingly said, "We should release him, as we owe him a debt and could give him a pass." Walt smiled but wanted to know if the uniform police obtained any additional information from Mr. Park.

"He is a bartender at a luxury hotel down near Central Park. He has another job too, as a private security guard. Shit on days off, he works at a late-night bowling alley over in the Bronx." His wife, Rosemary, was a secretary to a big shot investment banker on Wall Street, and together, they earned a pretty penny. So money, the cause of most domestic disturbances did not immediately seem to be the problem. "What about jealousy?" said Walt. "Her job paid almost as much as all three of Park's other jobs?" Walt said that he would review his finances but wanted to find the motive, as no one really believed this was an accident.

Walt spent time at the apartment with the police photographers taking pictures and taking the body of Rosemary Park to the morgue. Stephen and Rosemary kept meticulous files and everything was in order. While they lived just under their means, they had savings, nice clothing, and no real outstanding debt that Walt could discover. Walt wanted to like the guy and wanted to believe him but felt he was being lied to, and therefore questioned him again.

Now Stephen was in a holding cell at the 34th Precinct, and, as per usual protocol, his belt and shoelaces were removed to prevent him from committing suicide. He was looking down at his feet, and yet keeping his composure and posture as a good marine would do. Walt started to talk to him, not about the killing, but about his experience in World War II. Park explained that he was involved with the retaking of the Philippines in early 1945, and saw lots of combat. He was captured by the Japanese and released at the end of the war. He saw action in Korea as he led his men on an amphibious assault in Inchon during the Korean War. The more Walt heard, the more he liked the guy. "Why not confess?" Walt said, "Get a second-degree murder rap, serve five years, and you'll be home free." Park looked at his feet, and repeated the same story about his wife in the shower while he was cleaning the bayonet. Walt interjected and said, "Who the fuck cleans his bayonet in the bedroom on a Sunday morning while their wife is in a shower, you fucking liar?!" Park became silent, and Walt went over to Sergeant Skinner and said to give him the third degree to see if that would help make him talk.

Prior to the Miranda Decision, which established a code of conduct for police interrogations of criminal suspects held in custody in 1966, suspects could be "coerced to confess." This varied from sleep deprivation and non-stop questioning, to being slapped and occasionally punched. Walt went home that night with the case bothering him, as he could not understand why this former Marine captain would not admit to a lesser second-degree murder for a lovers' spat, and - heck, with his war records - could possibly be out of prison in three years. It just didn't make sense.

The next morning, Walt went into the station to interrogate Park again, and found him to be a total mess. His eyes were swollen, and his lips split. The nose was caked with blood and was now broken. Walt said, "What happened here?" An older detective, whose name was Munson, was seated near the detention cell. He said that the boys were taking him to the interrogation room when he fell down the precinct's stairs, and unfortunately suffered some injuries. Walt was angry and said, "I told you to give him a third-degree but not to beat the living shit out of him! However, what did you learn?" Walt asked, seemingly in disgust. "Nothing; he clammed up. He took a hell of grilling and said nothing. It almost seemed like love taps," Munson exhaled in a disappointed tone. "Maybe, we need to get Snider in when he gets off of patrol? No one can last 15 minutes with him," Munson stated. "Like hell, you will," said Walt, "He is my prisoner and my responsibility."

Park was a man about five feet and eight inches tall and a muscular 160 pounds. He was battered, bruised, and defiant. Walt asked him if he would like a drink of water, and he nodded in the affirmative. "Why didn't you talk?" asked Walt. Park said that he did, but when he again told the story about the "accident," fists and feet started flying. Walt admired the quiet confidence that Park portrayed, but like the other cops, wanted to get to the bottom of what really happened.

"Are you hungry, Mr. Park?" Walt asked the prisoner. "A little; I swallowed a tooth, but it wasn't filling," Park laughed, and Walt belatedly caught the joke. "Perhaps I can arrange something for you to eat rather than shoe leather that you have been getting; wait a minute." Walt spoke with Sergeant Skinner and, five minutes later, returned to Park, still hunched over on his stool in the tiny holding cell. Walt took a key and opened the cell door and removed the handcuffs off Park. "Do you agree to come out with me peacefully for breakfast, and if you try to escape, you will get a bullet in the back?" Park said, "I promise." Walt told him to go into the toilet and wash up first. After five minutes, they both walked out of the precinct house and went to a local coffee shop, which served breakfast around the corner.

Walt was surprised how hungry Park was as he devoured the bacon, over-easy eggs and toast in a matter of a minute. Walt said, "Do you want another order?" Park politely said, "Yes." Walt ordered another round for Park, while he asked for a black coffee for himself.

They sat and talked at the small booth, which had red leather seats that seemed to have been absorbing grease, cola, coffee, and tea since the 1920s. They talked about everything except the current case. Walt was fascinated by Park's war stories, both in World War II, and more recently in Korea. The guy, once you got to know him, was hard to dislike. He seemed to have been popular with his men in the Marines. From Walt's calls to Parks' employers, he was well liked, a hard worker, and very diligent.

Walt commented that he was sorry the cops went overboard while he went home, and warned they might do it again to get Park to talk. Park responded that he wasn't afraid of any beating the police would administer, as the Japanese captured him in the Philippines. There was nothing a New York cop could do to him that the Japanese interrogators didn't do to him during the war. The cops' beatings were like "a walk down Fifth Avenue," said Park with a smile. This impressed Walt, and he told Park so.

It was noon and they were still talking, now like old friends rather than a detective and a prisoner. Walt said, "How about lunch? We haven't eaten for an hour." Park smiled and said, "Sure." They both ordered hamburgers, medium well, plain, no ketchup or mustard.

When the burgers were served, Walt took a bite, swallowed and said, "Why did you kill her?" Park also took a bite out of his hamburger and said, "We were married just before I went to Korea in 1950. It was lust at first sight for both of us. Rosemary was everything a man could want - attractive, sexy, good in bed, and intelligent. I thought I was the luckiest man in the world."

Walt said, "Sounds good. What happened next?" "When I got my first leave from Korea, everything was the same, but yet felt different. I could not put my finger on it, but something wasn't right. I thought it was me, but before long, I went back for my second tour of duty. I came back and the feeling of estrangement was still there, although she said all the right things. After the war and my discharge from the Marines, we talked about saving up and moving to California to start a new life together on the West Coast."

"At first, I thought she was on board but noticed she preferred to stay in New York City. Strange since her parents now resided in Costa Mesa, California, and she got on well with them. I also noticed that she had to work late a lot at her company down on Water Street, near Wall Street. Then came weekend projects, and then came the need to accompany her boss on business trips to Washington DC, Boston, and Chicago. I smelled a rat, and one weekend, I told her I was going to work, but instead I followed her to work. However, she did not go downtown but traveled by train to New Rochelle, just outside of the city. There, she was met at the train station by her boss, who gave her the most passionate kiss I have ever seen. I felt like the smallest piece of shit that ever existed on the earth."

Park continued, "For months, I thought about this. At first, I planned to liquidate her boss, but then decided that it wasn't his fault entirely; she is gorgeous and unintentionally flirtatious. That's why I loved her so much. I finally decided to waste her, as I did not want to divorce her, as another man would have her. If I could not have her, then no one could have her."

"I thought about it day and night. At times, I just got cold feet. The other day, she got a call from her boss, who had to work Sunday. She seemed excited and said she needed to take a shower, get dressed, and go downtown to meet him to work on a brand new project. I saw red," said Park, "When she came out of the shower I plunged the same bayonet I killed the enemy with, straight into the heart of my wife, former soul mate, and lover. She looked at me as she was dying, and I swear she knew I knew, and even managed a smile. I closed her eyes, put her on the bed, kissed her one last time, and called the police."

Park asked Walt, "What happens next?" Walt told him in all honesty, "You will be tried on first-degree murder and will need a really good lawyer." Park nodded and asked if he could finish the burger and coke before going back to the 34th Precinct to be processed. Walt agreed. On the way to the station, they talked about boats, cars and airplanes, and nothing about the case. Park, in his own way, seemed at ease with the situation. Walt sensed his total acceptance of his fate.

Once back in the station, Walt gave the police and detectives clear instructions not to hurt his prisoner, and he told Sergeant Skinner that Park had a confession to first-degree murder.

In less than a year, Stephen Park was tried and convicted of first-degree murder of his wife, Rosemary Park. He was sent to Sing Sing maximum-security prison to await execution. Walt thought no more about this case until he heard from Park's lawyer, Sid Berkowitz, an above-average criminal attorney based near the 34th Precinct. Park said through Berkowitz that he was to be executed in three days, and asked Walt to attend the execution. Park's family abandoned him during the trial, and he wanted to see one friendly face before being put to death.

Walt agreed and traveled to Sing Sing prison with Berkowitz on the day of the execution and visited Park. Park said to Walt, "Thank you for everything." Walt said, "I arrested you and had you convicted; why would you thank me?" Park said, "You listened to my story, did not judge me, and treated me fairly and humanely throughout the process." They shook hands, and then Park was strapped into the electric chair. After the warden read his sentence, he nodded to the executioner who dispatched him into eternity.

Walt said he made it a point to attend the execution of any prisoner he caught who was convicted and sentenced to death. This was his only case where he felt some remorse, not because Park did not deserve to die - he did, but because, if circumstances had been different, Stephen and Rosemary would have had a spectacular life together - a total waste of two lives. He felt sad and told this to Berkowitz during their long drive together back to New York City.

Not all murders ended with confessions and arrests. During Walt's short tenure on the waterfront, he had a taste of frustration and failure to balance his recent good "collar" in the 34th Precinct.

Chapter 16

Murder on the Waterfront - An Unsolved Mystery

The 6th Precinct was down by the infamous New York City waterfront located in lower Manhattan. The area was known for the down-and-outs seamen from all nationalities who, in all likely circumstances, were not the most upstanding citizens of their respective countries. Walt referred to the merchant seamen as 20th century pirates, while other cops saw these individuals as the scum of the earth. However, there was no doubt that they worked hard, and when in the Port of New York in the early 1950s, they wanted to let off some steam.

Walt got a call to go to a freighter, which was docked in lower Manhattan, as there was a fatality on the ship.

"What the hell is this?" Walt asked Sergeant Warner. "Is this a homicide, suicide, or just a guy with a bad ticker?"

"How the hell do I know?! The son-of-a-bitch on the telephone could barely speak English and said something about a fatality.

Probably an accident, but check it out and let us know if you need backup."

Walt drove down to the dock, which stunk of dead fish, sewage, oil, and other God-knows-what pollutants in the toilet they called New York Harbor. The ship was a beaten up Eastern European-registered vessel. As Walt walked up to it, he smelt the stench of a sickeningly sweet aroma, which dove into his memory of some of the Russian-Jewish homes he had officially and unofficially visited in New York, and identified it as a particularly evil rendition of Borshch, or Russian beet soup. This, along with the other aromas the wharf gave off, made him feel a bit nauseous.

He walked up the gangplank and was greeted by a Slovak giant who, in broken English, said, "What do you want? Get Off." Walt flashed his gold detective shield and said, "New York Police; where is the captain?" The man stood still trying to process what Walt just said. "Asshole, take me to the captain or get the fuck out of the way." The giant moved, still pondering what was said but sure that the badge meant Walt had the authority to be there.

Walt climbed a rusty ladder toward the poorly painted ship's bridge, and identified the ship's mate, who had a black, grayish beard and longer than average hair. He was unkempt, but had a blue jacket with a gold band, so he must have had some rank or rate position of the ship, perhaps first mate or chief engineer. Walt asked for the captain, and the man laughed. "What's so funny? Walt asked the mate. "Don't you know? Captain Pavloff is dead. Found him in his stateroom this morning." "How did he die?" Walt asked. "Maybe lack of life," laughed the mate. Walt told him to take him to the cabin, and the mate answered, "Of Course." "What's your name?" Walt barked. He said, "Yuri." "Yuri what?" "Yuri Ossipov, Chief Engineer, at your service." He smiled and extended his hand, but Walt ignored it and walked on past him.

The cabin was dirty, not just untidy but filthy. It smelled of piss and sweat with a splash of vodka. The captain was on top of the unkept blankets and looked fast asleep. Walt almost did not want to disturb him but put his hand on his neck and did not feel a pulse. He was cool to the touch and when Walt picked up his arm, it was not too supple but beginning to stiffen with rigor mortis.

"What time did you find him?" Walt asked. "Just an hour ago," said the engineer. "When did you dock?" "Last night around midnight." "Was the captain on the deck then?" "Well, no... I can't remember, as it was foggy, and we were all at our stations as we docked. I am an engineer and was below the deck. Some of the crew would know." "Wouldn't the captain be required to dock the ship?" Walt asked. "Yes, but you know that the first mate, if the captain is drunk, can dock the ship."

"How many are in the crew?" asked Walt. "Twenty-seven, but now twenty-six without the captain," and he laughed again. "Did you like the captain?" Walt asked. "No," said the mate, "but nobody did." "Who in the Merchant Marine likes the captain?" he added, more as a statement rather than a question. Walt called for assistance to move the body and to start a process to interview the crew. While the captain had no real signs of injury, and it may have been a heart attack, he thought he could see some very faint bruises around the neck, and it appeared as if the captain may have had a bloody nose just before passing away. "Probably nothing, but maybe something," Walt thought.

Back at the 6th Precinct, Sergeant Warner wanted to know what Walt was thinking, and Walt hinted there might be foul play. Warner replied it isn't worth getting too involved with this and said, "These scumbags are all pirates anyway, and who cares if they kill one another out at sea." Walt agreed but said, "If Captain Pavloff was killed, it was probably in New York Harbor, perhaps at the dock; it is therefore our jurisdiction and our problem." Warner seemed a little annoyed, and Walt just ignored his feelings and ordered two other policemen to take statements at the ship.

Walt got two pieces of news later that day. One was that the captain was not only disliked but despised by most, if not all, the crew. Also, the medical examiner said that Pavloff died due to suffocation, probably smothered by a soft material like a pillow. "Shit," thought Walt, "We got a homicide and twenty-six suspects."

Walt was informed by Captain Al Bryson, a twenty-five-year veteran of the force who worked his way up the ranks from patrolman, "a cop's cop" who was tough but fair, that the SS Odessa had unloaded its cargo and would pick up new cargo to continue its voyage; it was due to leave New York City at 4 am tomorrow. This gave Walt fewer than sixteen hours to solve the case. Walt said that he could get a judge's order to hold the ship in port. Bryson said, "Yes, it is possible, but no one gives a shit about a drunk and now dead Ukrainian captain, and neither should you."

Walt returned to the ship to re-question Chief Engineer Ossipov. "What was the purpose of your visit to New York?" "To deliver canned fish and animal products, including canned hams and other culinary delights," smiled Ossipov. "What goods are you receiving for shipment today?" asked Walt. Ossipov said, "Flour, sugar, and other agricultural products." "Where was your last port of call?" Walt asked. "It is all in the ship log, but we were in Istanbul and came to New York via Marseille," said Ossipov. The internal alarms within Walt went off; "Heroin," he thought. Walt called the 6th Precinct and asked to track the cans of fish, meat, etc., as they may contain "product." He also formally asked for a judge's order to hold the ship until the investigation was complete.

Meanwhile, Walt invited Ossipov down to the precinct house for further questioning. Ossipov demurred, saying that he had to prepare for departure, but Walt said, "If you do not come with me, I will get a warrant for your arrest." Ossipov went with Walt reluctantly.

At the station, the mood was different. Walt could not put his finger on it, but when he asked for a room to interrogate Ossipov, Sergeant Warner and a vice plainclothesman wanted to join the session. "The more the merrier," said Walt.

Usually, in these situations, the police would take turns wearing the suspect down and trying to trip him up. However, in this case, Walt felt the tables were turned, and the questions they asked Ossipov were "softball," and at times, they seemed to answer Walt's questions on behalf of Ossipov. Walt was convinced that by reading the statements from the crew, Ossipov had the respect of the crewmen and became convinced that nothing would have happened to Captain Pavloff without Ossipov's knowledge.

Around midnight, Walt called Captain Bryson at home and after being told off for disturbing Bryson's wife, kids, and his beauty sleep, Walt requested permission to charge Ossipov with the first-degree murder of Captain Pavloff. Bryson raised his voice and started telling Walt that this was really not his business to get into, and that he needed to rethink the case. Walt also asked Bryson for a court order to hold the ship in port for at least 48 more hours. Bryson said he would do what he could but no promises. However, he instructed Walt to return Ossipov back to the ship in case his request was denied. "We do not need trouble with the State Department regarding this crappy investigation."

Walt slowly processed Ossipov out of the holding cell and walked him to the entrance of the station. He offered Ossipov a ride to the ship, which was about 10 minutes away, as it was pushing almost 2 am. Walt took the scenic route to see if he could glean any additional information about the case. Ossipov did say through tiredness or arrogance, "Things happen from time to time, but they always work out in the end." Walt said, "What do you mean by that?" Ossipov laughed and added, "Detective, we are all on the same team. We are all paid by the same boss. Are you naive, or are you a genius? I am afraid we will not meet again, but hope the powers to be will be kind to you." With that, Ossipov exited the car and walked slowly toward the ship. He mounted the gangplank and looked toward Walt and waved. He entered the ship and Walt never saw him again.

Walt drove like a maniac back to the 6th Precinct to see if he got a court order to hold the SS Odessa. When he arrived, the desk sergeant informed him that Captain Bryson called and said Judge

Rothstein denied the request to hold the ship; the Odessa was free to resume its voyage. Walt drove down to the waterfront and watched the gangplank go up, and the tugs ease Odessa away from the dock and out to the harbor and into the Atlantic. This was a kick in the head, as Walt was sure he had the right guy - Ossipov, possibly assisted by that "fucking giant" he saw when he first arrived on the scene.

Walt thought, "Was Pavloff purely hated, or were they shipping heroin and Pavloff got greedy? Did Ossipov get greedy? What strings were pulled in New York to get the ship out to sea ASAP?"

Walt heard that the Soviet Union rejected the body of Captain Pavloff, and he was buried in a pauper's grave. Walt was quickly reassigned from the 6th Precinct to the 24th Precinct, far from the fun of the waterfront. A mystery that remained unsolved, and one that bothered Walt to the end of his life.

Walt's next big break was a case in Harlem proper. As a detective, he did not like to leave cases open like the one with Captain Pavloff; however, due to lack of manpower or political will, this almost happened again while sent to assist the 28th Precinct.

Chapter 17

Homicide in Harlem - Solved

Working in the 24th Precinct didn't always mean you had duty in your own geographic area. The nearby 28th Precinct in Harlem proper was always stretched, even in the mid-1950s. Because of holidays, illnesses, or an influx of cases at times, the precincts in nearby areas needed to help, and usually, detectives and patrolmen were happy to help. One day, Walt was asked if he would mind going to the 28th for a murder. "A murder. I'd even consider going to New Jersey for a murder," joked Walt. He relished the chance to assist his brethren at the old 28.

Walt was told to visit an address just off 125 Street and walk up to the second floor where the body was. In the small, dingy, one-bedroom, one-bath apartment in a beaten up and subdivided brownstone building, Walt heard the barking sound of cops shouting orders from a mid-floor apartment. As usual, the walk up the steps was not without the broken lights, garbage thrown all over the floor, and the horrible smell of urine, vomit, and human feces.

An equally gruesome sight welcomed him when he arrived on the second floor, where he saw what looked like congealed blood in an oval pattern extending from inside the apartment to the hallway floor. Walt saw an average-built black woman, apparently in her mid-thirties, lying on the floor with her eyes wide open and an expression of horror frozen on her face. She had what looked like a light green nurse's uniform on. It seems she had her throat cut between the kitchen and the main door, as if she was trying to get out.

As he tried to step over the body into the flat, he felt his shoe stick to the floor into the semi-liquid blood that oozed out of the woman's body. "She was stabbed at least twice in the chest before the killer cut her throat," said one policeman. "I think she was a nurse." "Maybe some fucking junky did this?" said another patrolman at the scene. Walt checked her purse lying on the floor and discovered an identification card for a nearby hospital. He also found a purse with 11 dollars and some change. "Usually," Walt said, "if the motive is robbery, regardless of the amount, the robber takes the money and doesn't leave it in the purse." The older patrolman repeated, "A fucking junky must have thought she had drugs. We will never find him. An open and shut case, but this case is closed." "Shut the fuck up," Walt said and then asked if there were any witnesses to the killing. "Nothing; no sounds at all. An old lady next door noticed what she thought was tomato juice under the front door, but she then realized it was blood and called the police. That was two hours ago." One younger patrolman came out of the bathroom and said it didn't look like the vanity mirror was disturbed; if a junky did this, they would have ransacked the apartment for drugs. "Was she married, living with someone, or single?" asked Walt. "The woman, Debra Brown, was 38 years old and divorced for some ten years. She has an 18-year-old daughter at CCNY studying medicine," said the young police officer. "You are almost sensible. What's your name?," asked Walt with a smile. "Michael Berry," the patrolman said. "How long have you been on the force?" "Almost three years, but I want to be a detective," said Berry. "Don't we all?" said Walt, but he liked him, as he was looking to solve the murder and not just completing paperwork to get him home early.

Walt went back to the 28th Precinct with statements from neighbors and the first policemen on the scene. On the surface, it looked like a tough case, but he started by speaking with the daughter and the employers. As expected, Sharon Brown, Debra's daughter, was devastated. Her mother meant everything to her and was her inspiration to become a medical doctor. Walt tried to find out if Debra was seeing any man, or if the ex-husband lived nearby. "My father, the last I heard, was living in Atlanta." Walt was able to get a number for the ex-husband, and, a small miracle, was able to make contact with him on the first call. The man, Cecil Brown, said he had not seen his wife or daughter for almost five years, and he was a porter at a historic downtown hotel in Atlanta.

"Well, one suspect cleared," thought Walt.

Back at Debra's apartment, Walt searched for clues. From experience, he found that one of the the best clues for a murder case was a personal phone book. However, this wasn't readily available. There was nothing but some old receipts, a mixture of dirty and clean clothing, and a quasi empty icebox with a pint of bad milk, a shriveling apple, and a half bottle of gin. "Not a healthy diet," thought Walt, "but hey, she is dead now, so maybe she should have had the privilege of finishing the gin before she died." He stooped down and looked under the bed, behind the beaten-up dresser, and under the thread-worn throw rugs. Nothing, nothing interesting, not even remotely. He went into the living room and sat down as cops were putting away cameras and packing up other crime detection equipment, which littered the kitchen. The body was unceremoniously put into a body bag to be taken to the morgue. "No clues, no weapon, no witnesses, no nothing," thought Walt.

Walt had a habit of walking the crime scene one more time, and as his eyes scanned the kitchen, and the sickeningly sweet smell of blood assaulted his nostrils, he saw something he totally missed before. On the dirty white wall, all around the telephone attached to the wall, were telephone numbers written in pencil. Most were local, but some had area codes. Some were almost illegible, but most could be copied. Walt hit paydirt. He took out his notebook and started to copy one after another. Two numbers he recognized were Debra's ex in Atlanta, and the other was her daughter's number at the dorm at CCNY. Walt smiled and said to the one remaining policeman, "Now I will let my fingers do the walking," and exited the apartment to go back to the detective's office at the 28th Precinct and start his telephone campaign.

Back at the station, Walt used a blackboard to keep track of every number he called. He started with numbers nearest to the telephone as he copied them down at Debra's apartment.

He got the butcher, the baker, and the tailor, and still, he called. He then called a number which could have been interesting, a law firm. It seems that Debra's ex was behind in alimony, which she needed for school fees for Sharon. However, the sad fact was that Cecil Brown did not make a lot of money, and he was in a relationship down south, and what little cash he had gone to his new family first. Besides, Walt confirmed that it was not physically possible for Cecil to have committed the crime and get back to Atlanta. Also, Cecil did not seem to have a real motive. Yes, he was behind in alimony but did not seem to get worked up about it. He also seemed genuinely sad to hear Debra was dead. Walt put him as a maybe, but in his mind, he thought, "Probably not."

He was able to call Debra's minister, Reverend Anderson, who at first seemed a little unhelpful but told Walt that Debra attended a service a few Sundays ago, and a man in a delivery van stopped after church and spoke with her. "What did they talk about?" Walt asked. "I don't exactly know," said the mature sounding minister, "but I think they were having an argument." "What about?" Walt asked quickly. "Don't remember, but you know, young folks always seem to argue about love or money," he chuckled. "Yes, love and money," the minister repeated, and Walt thanked him and hung up. "A lead, a little sketchy, but worth following up," thought Walt.

Walt called numbers that were not answered and some just hung up, especially when he identified himself as a police officer.

Walt knew if the murderer was to be captured, he would need to move quickly, as a case like this gets cold fast and soon becomes virtually unsolvable. Debra Brown was just a regular resident of Harlem, and not a political figure or gangster. The fact appeared in Walt's face that he was already getting pressure to turn the case over to more inexperienced plainclothesmen, who, along with other cases, become just a statistic in some inspectors' reports downtown. The hard fact is, except maybe for Sharon and now Walt, nobody cared. Period.

Walt enlisted help though. He spoke with the desk sergeant and got Patrolman Michael Berry, the twenty-five-year-old from Pelham in the Bronx, as his assistant, at least for a few days. Berry was thrilled that Walt asked for his help and eagerly took half Walt's phone numbers and started dialing for dollars, hoping to find a delivery company. On day one, nothing, but they were down to nineteen numbers, which were not answered or where people hung up. The blackboard was filling up, but mostly with alibis and no real suspects. Berry still felt he would like to interrogate Cecil Brown, but Walt refocused him on the unanswered phone numbers.

The next day, Walt got a couple of men who said they knew or, in one case, dated Debra. Walt wanted to speak with them and arranged interviews that morning. Berry, in the meantime, got a laundry delivery company that occasionally called Debra Brown a customer. Berry looked forward to telling Walt when he returned from his interviews. Walt turned up just after 12 noon at the 28th, and Berry asked how Walt's interviews went. "Inconclusive, but making headway," said Walt. Berry could not hold in his excitement as he told Walt that he found a laundry delivery company in Harlem that had Debra Brown on their client list. Walt said, "Let's pay them a visit," and Berry eagerly agreed.

Off they went to the company only 15 blocks away. They were mildly disappointed that the firm had a tiny storefront, but once inside, the sound of laundry machines and dryers shook the reception room. An overweight black woman, in her late forties, knew they were cops before they introduced themselves. "Leave us alone; we ain't doing nothing wrong," she said. Walt laughed and said, "How do you know we are cops?" "Two white men with a bulge under the coat; you are cops or mafia, and you look too nice to be mafia," she said with a large kind smile. "What can I do for you, gents?" she asked. "My name is Martha Jones; we have the whitest sheets in town," she said with pride. Walt said he wanted to know how many drivers they employ. She said, "Two - Richard Stevens and Thad Green. Both are working right now making deliveries."

Walt said, "How old are they?" "Richard is 35, while Thad is merely a youngster at 21." "Do you know if they had any relationship with Debra Brown?" She replied, "I don't know, nor do I care. Live and let live, I say." Walt said that he was involved with homicide, and the problem was not living, it was dying that he was investigating. She gave Walt the delivery route for the day for both men and Walt said to Berry, "We can question them both, but my hunch is we start with Richard."

At a small hotel on 119th Street, where rooms are rented to pimps, whores, and junkies on an hourly basis, Walt and Berry asked the receptionist if the laundry delivery had occurred yet. "No," she said, without making eye contact and said, "We do not want trouble here." Walt said, "If you didn't want trouble, you would close this shooting gallery and whore house." The woman did not acknowledge what he said and actually pretended not to have heard him. They waited on a flea-bitten sofa, trying not to sit directly on the stains of God knows what on the fabric. They did not wait long when an average-built black man in a green delivery uniform came to the counter with a neatly wrapped package. He looked at Walt and Berry sitting down, dropped the package and headed for the door. Walt knocked a heavy standing cigarette reception ashtray in front of Stevens, which temporarily blocked his escape. He was agile and raced up the stairs of the hotel with Berry and Walt in full pursuit.

He ran to the end of the second-floor hall and proceeded to make his way out the window and onto the fire escape. Berry started to pull his .38 Special, but Walt said, "No; we want him alive." Stevens was not only agile, but he was as fast as a gazelle and sprinted down an alley toward some looming tenements in the hope of finding an open door, garage, or just a window. He was out of luck and trapped in the courtyard. He tried to get through a gap between Walt and Berry but was tripped, and as he tried to get up, Walt gave him a hard uppercut into the tip of the jaw. Berry followed up instantaneously with a right cross to his left cheek, and he was down for the count.

"I didn't do anything," Stevens said as Walt pulled him up. "What didn't you not do?" Walt said. Stevens was looking to sprint again, and he took another sock in the jaw by Walt, which again sent him onto the dirty garbage-covered alley. He was bleeding from his mouth and nose, and he seemed to understand that he would not be getting away, at least not today. They arrested him and took him back to the 28th Precinct.

Once there, Stevens finally admitted that he both knew, and occasionally dated, Debra Brown. He said he was aware that she had been saving money for her daughter's education, and that she did not trust banks and kept the money at home. Walt asked what happened next. He said that she sensed he was not really interested in her but in her savings, and she dropped him like a hot potato. Walt asked what happened next. He went to see her on the morning of the murder, but he didn't want to kill her, just scare her to get the money. He said she reluctantly let him in when he told her he missed her, but once inside, he grabbed her and told her to give him the savings. She said she only had about 10 dollars in her purse, and he told her, "Bullshit; give me the savings!" "She told me she gave it to her daughter for tuition and that she did not have it. I searched the place with her, and then asked her where her daughter was staying and to call her, as we were going to see her now. Debra then pushed me and almost knocked me to the ground. I recovered and stabbed her, as I was scared she would get the knife from me. After stabbing her twice, she still sprinted for the door, and out of plain fear and anger, I blanked out and must have cut her throat, but I do not remember this happening. I ran out of her apartment as fast as I could and didn't look back. I really didn't mean to kill her; I just wanted the money. Times are hard, you know."

Walt, assisted by Patrolman Michael Berry, were both given special commendations for solving this case. This was the boost

Berry needed to get into the detective division, and Walt got the satisfaction of catching the killer of Debra Brown. While he was internally delighted by the result of the case, Walt felt he needed to have one final meeting with Sharon Brown to let her know that her mother's love for her was so great, she died protecting her daughter from Stevens. Sharon was grateful for Walt's update and attended the ceremony at the police department when Walt and Berry were given their commendations.

Walt was able to settle down in the 24th Precinct; however, he told his story about an encounter with a former policeman who did not quite know when to call it quits.

Chapter 18

There's a Ghost In Spanish Harlem

The 24th Precinct in the mid-1950s was responsible for an area known as Spanish Harlem. The area was a mix of mostly poor or working-class Puerto Ricans, African-Americans, and elderly Caucasians, who did not or could not exit the area just after World War II during the Great White Flight. The area was tough, as gangs of youths - such as portrayed in the Rodgers and Hammerstein's play "West Side Story" - roamed the streets to mark and defend territory from encroaching gangs from nearby neighborhoods, generally making a nuisance of themselves with small shop owners and law-abiding residents in the general area who were forced to remain in the neighborhood.

Cops then were also tough and more than one old Irish police sergeant would say that the end of a nightstick or truncheon was the best attitude adjuster and lie detector around. In order to maintain law and order, cops needed to be not liked but respected. Tough love consisted of lots of arrests, especially teenage males, occasional shootouts where a majority of the perpetrators were on the wrong end of the cop's gun, and plenty of ass-kicking, which would be followed up with an arrest for assaulting a police officer. Things were simpler in those days, and order was just about maintained, but trouble was always simmering just beneath the surface.

Walt mostly avoided all of this, as he was now a detective and traded in his tin badge for a prestigious gold shield. This was what he always dreamed of, and he had more than his share of cases investigating robberies, burglaries, assaults, rapes, and of course, murders. He worked with two other detectives in the precinct and, as a relatively young detective, was making his mark with excellent "collars," which were arrests that normally resulted in convictions. He said he didn't particularly like this area, as he and his new wife lived in Riverdale in the Bronx, but he was now a detective and not bored at all, except one day on a crisp autumn evening.

To set the scene, things were changing in the 24th Precinct, as the original police station built just prior to the American Civil War was being closed, and a new purpose-built police station was erected across the street. Until the old precinct house could be torn down, the police and civilian administrators used the old building as general storage for old files and equipment, but not weapons and such. The building was padlocked, and the Sergeant on duty had the only key. Occasionally, a policeman or administrator needed to access the building to store or look for old files. Still, it usually was unoccupied and virtually never used at night, as the electricity was turned off. Cops, in the dressing room, did, on occasion, talk about a creepy vibe and a feeling that they were being watched. More than one policeman, when locking up, heard footsteps upstairs when he knew there were no others in the building. Footsteps on the stairs and cell doors of the old jail squeaking and sometimes slamming. "It is just the building settling," they would say. However, there was nothing more or less to these off occurrences until that one quiet Sunday night.

Walt was bored that cool evening with the prospect of re-reading weeks-old Life magazines and three-day-old newspapers. He did not like reading, but he hated being bored. He was the only detective on duty that shift, as no one expected much to happen and there were only four patrol cars on duty. All was exceptionally quiet, even for a Sunday night/Monday morning during this "graveyard shift." Walt, anticipating pure madness of doing nothing more than re-reading, asked Sergeant O'Rourke a favor. O'Rourke was a twenty-two-year veteran of the force, greying and in his early fifties, who spent most of his time thinking and talking about retirement, and moving the family to the Jersey Shore. Walt asked him if he would assign the next call to him, rather than a patrol car. This was, even in the 1950s, a bit unorthodox, since detectives should follow up and solve crimes, while patrolmen responded to calls for assistance. However, the sergeant took pity on the bored detective and agreed, however reluctantly, to the request.

Around 2 am on Monday, Sergeant O'Rourke came into the break room where Walt was scanning old magazine articles and nursing a cup of black coffee. "I got something if you want it, but it is really nothing at all.". Walt said "Anything is better than this toxic shitty coffee. What do you have?" "We just took a call from a woman next door who said she saw a light on the second floor of the old precinct house. I told her," O' Rourke continued, "that there is no electricity connected and asked her if she had been drinking. She said she wasn't drinking and the light was moving, so whoever it was had a flashlight or lantern." Walt's first reaction was it must be a cop, but O'Rourke said he has the only keys to the building, so maybe it was a break-in, some local kids hoping to find money or guns in the boarded-up and mostly unused building.

Walt said he would go, and ran out into the chilly November night before the Sergeant could change his mind and assign it to a patrol car. Walt had his flashlight with new batteries, and at first, he walked around the old precinct house looking for any signs of broken glass indicating a break-in. Nothing, which he found curious, and he looked up at the top windows and saw no light and wondered out loud if this was a practical joke by Sergeant O'Rourke, put up by the equally bored patrolmen that evening. However, he was out now. Maybe he could catch a burglar and make the night go by a little faster.

He took the master keys O'Rourke gave him and unlocked the padlock, which was attached to a thick iron chain around the building's old and original tarnished brass-door handles. He then took out a much older key and unlocked the large iron lock, which was fitted in the aging wooden door. The lock turned over with a lot of pressure from Walt, and the door opened with an eerie squeak, which echoed throughout the deserted building. There was scuffling on the floor as rodents and insects scurried around, as the light beamed from where Walt's flashlight illuminated the lower floor. "Is anybody here?" Walt shouted, still thinking a police officer may have managed to appropriate a spare key, and be in the building catching up on paperwork. However, Walt's voice echoed through the almost totally empty building. He moved inside and slammed the heavy wooden doors shut, and when he did that, he felt the vibration of the doors closing through the very soles of his shiny black Oxford shoes.

Again, he shouted, "Is anyone here?" hoping this time it would spook a potential teenage thief into moving from his hiding spot, and then Walt could move in for the arrest. Again, once the echoing ceased, the old Civil War precinct house was as quiet as a tomb. Light from the streetlight outside filtered into the lower floor. It revealed shadows of broken desks and chairs, along with police cars' spare tires, and tools from the motor pool, which were temporarily housed in the dilapidated building. Walt made his way around the relatively small room, which was dominated by a large wooden desk elevated a couple of feet above the floor. This is where sergeants of the past oversaw their police officers prior to their patrol and signed in arrested suspects. Walt was thorough and checked the closets and under the large desk, hoping to find signs of an intruder but so far, no luck.

Before leaving the ground floor, he decided to go into the basement to see if somehow the intruder may be hiding in the old holding cells, which had housed prisoners since the Civil War. He opened the sturdy but beaten up wooden doors, still with some green paint attached precariously to the ancient wood. The hinges squeaked almost as loud as the main door as Walt started his noisy descent into the basement. He remembers when the station was operational a few months earlier; no one particularly liked going down these stairs. The lighting was poor with a few naked 60-watt bulbs, and the stairs sounded as if they would collapse at any moment. He knew if someone were downstairs and had a gun, he would be a sitting target. However, his flashlight betrayed no signs of life except a scurrying rat or two under the filthy brown rusted toilets and pipes in the holding cells.

Each cell was covered with graffiti of past prisoners who were housed here before transportation to court, and later to more secure prisons within and outside of New York City. As he checked each cell, he couldn't help chuckling at a carved bit of graffiti in one cell, which radiated the works "Fuck Abe L. CSA 63." This must have been carved by a captured confederate, perhaps during the riots of 1863, which forced the Union Army to withdraw valuable assets from the Virginia battlefields to put down the mayhem and looting during the middle of the Civil War. After checking the narrow closets and squashing a few plump and aggressive roaches, he made his way up the wobbly stairs and back to the ground floor.

"Two floors searched and two more to go," Walt thought as he climbed a slightly wider and more sturdy set of wooden stairs to the second floor. After shining his flashlight down the hall, he opened closed offices, which were filled with piles of files, papers of arrests from years gone by. Desks seem to sag under the weight of the countless files. Yet in every office, Walt checked under the desk and in the narrow closets looking for the elusive intruder, but after searching all six offices and one meeting room again filled with cardboard boxes, files and paper, he knew if anyone were in the building, they would be on the next, top floor.

Walt again yelled out, "Is there anyone here? Come forward!" Yet again, he was met with a chilling silence. As he climbed the creaking stairs, he thought he noticed a light spot on the entry platform on the third floor. Upon arriving at the landing, he looked down the short and narrow hall and saw light escaping under the door from the farthest office. At this point, he drew his .38 Detective Special, as, clearly, the light was too strong to be from a distant streetlamp. As he approached the door, which was partially open, he saw that the unnatural light was not made from a battery-operated flashlight but by the warmer, richer light from a lantern. He even heard the hissing of the fuel source as he pushed open the door quickly.

At the desk facing him about six feet away, was the figure of a man, about 50 years old, with brownish-grey disheveled hair and a distinguished mustache cut in a handlebar fashion. The man seemed annoyed and said gruffly, "What do you want?" Walt was surprised not only by the man but also by the authority in his voice. Walt said, "How did you get in and with whose permission?" The man sitting down pushed halfway back on his swiveling chair, and Walt could then see his blue uniform and brass buttons. He also saw sergeant stripes on his shoulder. The man said. "I am here by my own authority," with a tough Irish brogue, "and I will finish up in a couple of minutes." Walt told him he needed to leave with him and then go back next door to discuss this matter. The man said, "Fine; give me a couple of minutes to finish up here." Walt agreed, holstered his revolver, and decided to check the other closed offices to make sure no one was in any of them. He felt strange; something wasn't in place. Clearly, the man was a cop but he couldn't put his finger on it. As he checked the next-door office, Walt heard the man shuffling papers through the open doorway, but when he got back to the hallway, the light of the lantern was out, and the room was dark. This spooked him, as he did not hear footsteps and wondered if the man was, in fact, impersonating a police officer. He re-checked all the offices, closets, and meeting rooms throughout the entire building. He even re-entered the basement holding cells to see if the man was down there, but the station house was silent and very vacant. Walt was certain that he was alone and the man was now gone. "But how?" he thought.

As a detective, what do you do and what do you say when you thoroughly examined the whole building and there was no one alive in the old precinct house? Walt secured the locks in front of the station and walked across the street to the new 24th Precinct. Inside, Sergeant O'Rourke and two patrolmen were having coffee and shooting the breeze. "What did you find?" Sergeant O'Rourke asked Walt. He had to think fast and answered that there was a policeman, a sergeant, in the building, but he left while he was securing the area. O'Rourke laughed disparagingly, saying no one was in the building and questioned if Walt was taking the piss. Walt insisted a policeman was, in fact, in the building, but he could not identify who it was as his face wasn't familiar. The sergeant, who actually had a soft spot for the young detective, wrote in his evening report that an intruder was in the building but escaped just before the detective arrived. This should satisfy the captain when he reviews the weekly report.

Walt was perplexed, as he did not believe he was seeing things, but how could he rationalize in his mind what occurred? He hardly slept a wink when he got home to the Bronx in the morning. This is now an open case in the mind of the new detective.

The following week, when Walt transitioned to the day shift of 8 am to 4 pm, he was ordered by the precinct captain to give his account of what happened when he investigated the old precinct house. When Walt entered Captain John Crowe's office, he found him to be neutral, and perhaps even mildly friendly, but he was looking for a complete description of the intruder. Walt gave him the description sans uniform, and the captain nodded and said "Is that all?" While looking around the captain's office, Walt saw old black and white photographs of perhaps a dozen or more police officers from the 24th Precinct, who were killed in the line of duty. One photo, which Walt was drawn to like a paperclip drawn to a magnet, was of Sergeant Kennedy, who was shot and killed by an armed robber holding up a nearby jewelry store in the late 1880s. Walt's heart skipped a beat and Captain Crowe asked him what was wrong. Walt said, "Nothing is wrong; I was just thinking about something else." Captain Crowe then said, "Detective, it looks as though you have seen a ghost." Walt asked Captain Crowe if he knew anything about Sergeant Kennedy. Captain Crowe said, "Unfortunately, not much, but I heard from the old-timers that the man had a reputation of being diligent and was a well-respected leader amongst his men. Only the good die young, Walt," Captain Crowe said. "Why do you ask?" "He looks familiar and I wondered if his grandchildren were cops," Walt said quickly. Captain Crowe laughed and said, "I wouldn't know, as there are dozens of Kennedys in the NYPD. However, it would be great to have more men like Sergeant Kennedy on the force." Walt nodded in agreement, "It would be great indeed."

Walt stayed perplexed by this interaction with Sergeant Kennedy and wondered why he came back and why he showed himself to Walt. Walt's own explanation is that you couldn't keep a good man down, and perhaps the day Kennedy was shot, he had to finish up paperwork before going home. Nothing more or less, and Walt was a witness to both the diligence of this man addressing a very mundane matter - paperwork. Walt thought, "I Hope the afterlife offers more than eternally doing paperwork," and went next door for a decent cup of coffee.

While the encounter with Sergeant Kennedy was amiable, many other encounters were far less peaceful. Walt spoke about an occurrence which he had one Christmas Eve in Spanish Harlem.

Chapter 19

A Christmas Eve Shooting in Spanish Harlem

Walt was working on Christmas Eve in 1955. The old pre-Civil War 24th Precinct house was demolished to make room for a police parking lot. All the history, drama, and ghosts were now a memory of times long ago. However, this Christmas Eve would change Walt's perception of life much more than the strange encounter he had in the old precinct house a year or so before. This night to remember occurred with witnesses and ended with questions on right and wrong, and whether we all have guardian angels. This was a transition from innocence to "something else" and maybe, redemption.

On this unusual evening, all three detectives were working the midnight to 8 am shift. The reason for this was that, if you wanted to earn extra holiday time, the police union negotiated on behalf of the cops that an officer could get up to two full days off if they worked certain holidays. Since Walt and his partners wanted more time off in the summer and spring, why not work Christmas Eve, which was usually quiet and peaceful, even in Spanish Harlem?

Detectives Whittle and Perez were strapping men. Doug Whittle was six feet two and 240 pounds of pure muscle. He was smart and knew a lot about everything. He loved it when making an arrest the perpetrator resisted, and then he could use his infamous right-cross to take down the suspect. He wore a bland grey jacket, blue trousers, and a thick brown overcoat, which had a few stains from coffee with milk, and hamburger grease from lunches and dinners on the go while investigating cases.

Detective Raphael Perez stood an inch shorter at six feet one, with a slightly larger stomach than Whittle, but still strong and capable of handling any miscreant who tried to stop him from apprehending his suspect. Perez was the most religious man of the three; he looked forward to returning home the next morning and taking his two daughters and wife to Catholic mass after opening Christmas presents. He was a second-generation New Yorker whose parents were from San Juan, Puerto Rico, and he spoke Spanish fluently. He could deliver instructions to young gang members in Spanish or in English, which came in handy, especially in the 24th Precinct.

Walt was, funnily enough, the smallest one of the group. He stood at only six feet tall, and weighed just about 210 pounds. Not quite the same fighting weight nor physique than when he was in the US Army Air Corps during World War II. He started to show some signs of middle age with an extra inch or two around the waistline. His well-groomed full head of hair was still jet black without a hint of white or grey. Certainly, he was ready, able, and willing to stand up to any criminals or gang members, and usually, they came out of the situation worse than him.

As the night progressed, the detectives bombarded the Desk Sergeant with jokes, belches, farts, and the occasional spit wads and paper airplanes. They were just doing their time to earn a few extra days off and could care less about the traditional Christmas carols, which crooners sang over the AM radio stations. Sergeant Cohen, in the mid-1950s, was a relatively rare Jew on the police force, and a sergeant at that, and he was looking to catch up with his mandatory reports. He switched duties with Sergeant Riccio, who wanted to take Christmas Eve off to be with his family. Smiling while the detectives ran amuck in the mostly deserted station, Sergeant Cohen thought out loud, "How do I get these guys out of my hair so I can get something accomplished tonight?" It almost looked hopeless as he felt he would need to babysit until the morning shift arrived around 7:30 am.

Just after 3 am, a call came in from a woman who spoke "Spanglish," a mix of Spanish and English, and Cohen kept saying, "Where? Who? What? What's your address? Speak slowly and clearly, please. Alright, I will send someone right away." Cohen shouted and then slammed the phone back on the cradle, and the ringing sound of the phone vibrating sent a minor ripple through the precinct house. Cohen yelled out, "Which one of you assholes wants to break up a domestic disturbance?" The three detectives each said in unison "Me." Smiling slyly, Cohen then said, "Yeah, this is a great use of NYPD resources sending three detectives to break up one little lovers' spat. However," he added, "this is opportune, as I need to finish my weekly reports for the captain by 8 am, so by all means, all of you go to this address. It's only six blocks away; do me a favor and stay there until I go home." Everyone laughed, as this seemed like a win/win.

Walt was most eager, as he was hoping the guy, who was described as being five feet eight and 160 pounds and probably drunk, may be in the mood to mouth off to the detectives, and Walt could have a good ass-kicking session. However, Whittle and Perez were not going to be left behind and wanted to have some fun too. Besides, Whittle said that there was a 24-hour coffee shop and snack bar near that location, and maybe they were open on Christmas Eve, and just maybe they could all have a hot coffee and a stale donut or two after breaking up the disturbance.

As domestic arguments go, the appearance of the police usually calms things down, but sometimes the policemen become the target of rage for both the man and the woman, and you never know how things will work out. It was a very cold ten-minute walk from the station to the apartment building. The detectives had to walk slowly, as ice formed on the sidewalks and none of them had thought about wearing boots, as they really had not expected to be leaving the police station that night. Therefore, they were occasionally slipping as they struggled to move forward.

The building was typical for the area in the 1950s. From the outside, it was an old brownstone, three stories high, with a grand entrance, which was wide with white marble. It may have been a small hotel in the late 1890s to the 1920s when times were good, or at least better, in this area of Manhattan. Like in virtually all public housing structures, all lights had been vandalized and sure enough, the elevator was also not working. This meant they would need to walk up the wide tiled stairs to reach the third floor, where the argument was taking place. However, they did not hear any yelling, cursing, or anything at all, and the apartment building was quiet.

A full moon illuminated the lobby and white marble floors through windows on the doors, and the detectives were able to see the landing above each flight of stairs as they ascended toward the third floor. They walked across the stair still talking and starting to pant a little, as years of Duncan Donuts with Chock Full O' Nuts coffee and cream made the assent a little harder than it should have been.

As they turned on the final platform to ascend the last 11 steps to reach the third floor, the light from the moon was now partially blocked by a figure standing there facing toward the detectives. Walt noticed immediately that this individual seemed to match the height and body size of the man they wanted to speak with. He also was holding an object in his right hand. Immediately, Walt yelled, "DUCK!!" and with that, the roar of a gun firing at about 15 feet away, along with the accompanying bright flashes, made time stand still. As the detectives dropped to the stairs, they heard the bullets whiz over their heads, bodies, and ricochet with the insect-like sounds of bullets as they hit marble, stone, and metal.

Walt, Whittle, and Perez pulled out their .38 caliber Detective Specials, and each one opened fire on the assailant. The situation was surreal in that the suspect had an automatic weapon, probably a Colt 45 army surplus, as they did not hear the clicking sound of the revolver's magazine spin. Walt fired with adrenaline pumping, ears popping, and the acrid smell of gunpowder filling the hallway. He sensed the assailant was almost dancing as the detective's bullets were hitting him. Each detective emptied his revolver of six rounds while the assailant did the same. In total, twenty-six shots were fired. The assailant was shot seven times in the head, chest, and stomach. He died instantly.

As soon as the gunbattle ended, there was a wail of babies crying, women screaming, and men shouting and cursing in Spanish and English. While Perez and Whittle guarded the body and searched the area for accomplices, Walt entered the apartment where the man lived, and he saw a small and delicate Hispanic woman cowering on the couch, holding to protect an infant in her arms. The infant was screaming its lungs out. The woman had a bloody nose, swollen eyes, and a cut lip. She said her husband was drunk and he couldn't sleep, and he wanted to throw the baby out the window. She added that he did this occasionally, and when he sobered up, he did not remember and was really a good man. She then asked Walt what the noise and gunshots were all about, where Alvaro was, and if he was alright.

Walt told her to calm the baby down, and he picked up her phone and dialed for an ambulance and for the police. The patrol cars arrived in a minute or two and set up a perimeter around the man, who was pronounced dead on the scene. Once the woman started to calm the baby down, she went out into the hallway and launched into absolute hysterics, as she saw her husband lying in a pool of blood. This again set off the infant, and the other babies in other apartments started wailing in sympathy, but to a lesser extent than just after the gun battle. A big resident in boxer shorts came out of his apartment and yelled, "Shut the fuck up!" This made the crying even worse. Perez told him to shut the fuck up in Spanish or he would spend Christmas in jail; this did the trick.

Not one detective was hit despite being no more than 15 feet from the gunman. The assailant, Alvaro Cortez, was a former Military Policeman during World War II and received medals for marksmanship. He married right after the war to a 17-year-old neighborhood girl, Maria, who he got pregnant, and worked at various jobs, mostly custodial, and in most previous cases, was fired because of drinking, and at times, fighting with his co-workers.

As for Maria Cortez, Walt wasn't sure how she made out, other than her mother took her and her granddaughter in, and she soon became a nurse's aide at a nearby hospital. There was a grand jury investigation and the death was deemed justifiable. This was considered, in the police department, an open and shut case.

Walt remembered that during his drive home to his wife that Christmas morning, he was listening to the radio and this incident was on the news. He also remembered listening to Silent Night, sung by Nat King Cole. He felt the irony of it all.

In future years, in times of clarity, Walt would say that he felt an angel was with him, Whittle and Perez, that night. He also mentioned that although he knew in his heart that he did the right thing, he wondered how he would explain this on Judgement Day. How do you take another's life on Christmas Day, or any day for that matter? He hoped the Almighty was understanding. He told my brother and me that, "Taking a life, for whatever the reason, changes you somehow, and the change is not for the better."

He hoped that his two boys would never experience that feeling, as you lose your innocence. This always resonated with Roots and me during our entire lives.

Walt also remembered a shooting that did not end with a fatality. In fact, he was thanked for shooting but not killing the suspect's son. The story is ironic, yet sadly common, in the 24th Precinct in the mid-1950s.

Chapter 20
"Thank You for Not Killing My Son"

Not all shootings ended in a fatality. Sometimes, there was a turn of events that struck Walt as more than ironic, as opposed to the theory of a guardian angel. Yet, in a city and district where there was so much pain and suffering, Walt felt that sometimes, occasionally, God had a sense of humor, and if you were open enough, or tuned to the right frequency, you could get a glimpse of this cosmic humor.

An intriguing incident occurred toward the end of his tour of duty in the 24th Precinct. Walt was investigating an armed robbery at a pawn shop that was near the border of the 23rd Precinct in Harlem proper. As he was following up with a pistol-whipped 60-year-old Jewish pawn shop owner, who kept on repeating like a mantra, "I don't want to hurt anyone; I just want to help! What did I ever do to deserve this?" Walt heard a crash as an iron toaster smashed through a glass window on the fourth floor of a tenement building. The toaster broke into pieces as it just missed a pedestrian walking by the pawn shop. Next, the profanity flowed from the upstairs window, like water being forced from a broken faucet. It was violent, hateful, and full of rage. The tirade was directed at a woman, as the words, "You fucking bitch," were a part of this ceaseless stream of obscenities.

Walt ran through the lobby, and as it was early in the afternoon, mothers with their children, along with delivery men, were in his way as he pushed through the crowd and ran up the stairs. Out of breath, he stopped when he reached the landing on the fourth floor and listened to where the shouting was coming from. Halfway down the hall, through a closed door, he heard the commotion. Walt walked to the door and pounded on it, "Open up; this is the police!" The shouting ceased for a moment, but Walt heard the frantic sobbing of a woman inside. The door flung open and there was a black man, slightly shorter than Walt, about five feet ten, and much heavier and stockier. As a matter of fact, the man could almost fill the entire door frame. He appeared to be in his early thirties, and his well-groomed and short hair could not conceal the deep seething anger he was feeling.

"What the fuck do you want?" he shouted. Walt flashed his detective shield and said, "Did you throw the toaster out the window?" The man replied, as he pointed to an obviously battered 30-something-year-old thin and shabby-dressed black woman, "No, I threw it at that bitch, but unfortunately I missed her." The woman, who was curled up in a corner on the floor, was sobbing, "I'm sorry, I'm sorry, I will not do it again. I promise, I promise." The man turned to her and in an icy calm voice said, "I know you won't do it again, cause I'm going to kill you." He then turned slowly to Walt and said, "Go now, or I will have to kill you too. This bitch is fucking around while I am working, and I got to make things right." With that, Walt told him that he was under arrest and for him to get into the position, as Walt was going to take him to the police station. The man said with an even deeper voice, "Get out of here, as I don't want to kill you too, but will if you don't leave now."

With that, Walt made a tight fist and punched the man in the jaw with a lightning right cross as hard as he possibly could. The man barely flinched and even looked somewhat bemused. Walt followed with a swift uppercut again to the jaw, and it landed squarely under the chin. A tooth came tumbling out of the man's mouth, and he said in a cool and collective voice, "Now I am going to kill you first, then I will get to that bitch." He picked Walt up, as if he was a small trash can, and threw him, with ease, down the hallway. As Walt stumbled to get up, he was propelled backward to the opposite wall by a strong punch to his left side of the head. Walt knew he had to remain standing, or he was done for. The man reached back and threw another punch that Walt managed to duck, and it grazed but stung his head like the sting of a dozen bees.

Again, Walt knew he had to do something quickly, or he was finished, as the man was getting angrier by the second and his head was puffing up with a mixture of hate, anger, and perhaps high blood pressure. Reaching for his Detective Special .38 revolver, Walt backed up and instructed the man to put his hands on the wall and spread eagle. The man said, "Fuck You."

As the man came closer, Walt fired a shot at point-blank range into the man's right shoulder. He flinched and said, "Fucker, you are really getting me mad." Walt then fired the remaining five rounds into the man's chest as he came closer to Walt. The man paused and said, "I think I will lie down now." He then collapsed. Walt thanked his lucky stars that the guy was sitting in the public hallway, bleeding but retaining consciousness. Walt had one of the neighbors call the ambulance, who arrived quickly just as the sirens of police cars came to the front of the building.

The man and woman were taken to the hospital. She had a broken jaw, broken arm, and was missing several teeth. The suspect had six bullet wounds, yet none of them hit a vital organ, and he would survive.

The next day, Walt went to see the assailant who was being visited by an elderly, well-dressed black man, who turned out to be the man's father. The distinguished man took Walt's hand and said, "Thank you for not killing my son. My boy has a bad temper, and he believed his wife was cheating on him. My son Hector is really a good boy and is a moving man by profession, and a few years ago, when he was in better shape, an amateur boxer." Hector looked up from the hospital bed and said, "Detective, I am ashamed of my behavior, and I apologize for what I said and what I did. Thank you for not killing me." Hector's father added that he was a Baptist Minister, Right Reverend Jackson, who had been at a local church for ten years now, and always prayed that his son would hold his temper, but yesterday he just blew up.

In the aftermath, Walt continued to visit Hector in the hospital until he was well enough to be released from the hospital and remanded into custody. At the trial, Walt testified that although Hector beat his wife and assaulted a policeman, he seemed to see the error of his ways, and in a very unusual stance by Walt, asked the judge to show leniency to Hector Jackson.

Instead of 10 years in prison, Hector got three years, and from what Walt heard, he successfully reintegrated into the community after getting out of prison, and became a model son and member of the community. Hector's wife divorced him, and she moved back to North Philadelphia, where her family resided and hopefully found a more peaceful existence.

In another year, Walt, upon the birth of his first son, decided to give up his detective duties and take more regular hours as a patrolman. He also had the seniority to move to a precinct closer to home in the Bronx. This was Walt's "second tour of duty" as a patrolman, and as in the Chinese Consulate adventure, did not relish the idea of standing around during the World Series. However, in 1963, Walt had a dugout view of the games, but his interest was not really in the games at all.

Chapter 21

Walt at the 1963 World Series

October in the late 1950s and early 1960s meant something special to the officers and men of the 46th Precinct in the Bronx. It was time for baseball's World Series, and it was almost guaranteed that the New York Yankees would be participating in the event. While the Dodgers out in Brooklyn and the Giants in Manhattan occasionally made it to the World Series, the Yankees seemed not only to attend, but usually win these championship games. For Walt, this posed a problem. Since transferring back to uniform patrol in late 1959 and being reassigned closer to home in the Bronx, the World Series was one thing that annoyed Walt more than just about any other nuisance. Walt hated baseball and had zero interest in the sport. Neither did he like basketball, but he could tolerate, and go to, a football game. He did like ice hockey though, and would frequently see his beloved New York Rangers play in Madison Square Garden, and would also fork out good money to see professional boxing.

Every year, Walt was asked, as a senior patrolman, whether he wanted to guard the Yankee dugout or the Visitor dugout during the Yankee home games during the Series. He would jokingly answer, "Give me the parking lot patrol, as I may make a collar arresting a teenager breaking into a parked car, but I will not make an arrest in the Yankee dugout, even if a player steals a base." He was popular with the men, as he would always give a choice assignment to another patrolman who was dying to sit in the Yankee dugout during the World Series. He enjoyed being free to roam around and chat with fans, vendors, and businessmen who were hawking wares during the contest. This, however, changed in

1963 when the Yankees and the Los Angeles Dodgers played in the World Series.

The commanding officer, Captain Timothy Storm, addressed the men before the Series to assign the parking lot, stadium, and dugout positions. As the Yankees dugout was the prime spot, Walt, being a senior officer, got it. However, when Walt protested and said he wanted to change this assignment for the parking lot, Captain Storm smelt a rat and said, "I don't know what you are up to, but you will guard the Yankees dugout day one, and the Dodger Dugout day two." The other patrolmen groaned or snickered, as they knew Walt hated baseball and secretly wished they were given the plum assignment.

Walt did his best to convince the captain, but he was reminded that an order is an order, and he reluctantly agreed to arrive at Yankees Stadium two hours before game time to take up his post. On the first day of the World Series, the Yankees lost 5 to 2, and Sandy Koufax struck out the most Yankees ever during a World Series. However, Walt did not remember this. What he remembered was talking to Mickey Mantle and Whitey Ford between innings, about where they could get the best steak and Italian food in the Bronx, where the bars stayed open for extended hours, and where the prettiest girls attended "ladies' night." Walt knew all the restaurants and clubs, legal and otherwise in the Bronx, and Mantle and Ford valued this information. He remembered they were alright for baseball players, and they seemed thrilled to have a policeman not asking them about baseball. Whitey Ford joked with Walt and said, "Having a cop not ask us about baseball, or not asking for an autograph, is like a hooker taking non-sexual questions from a john."

On the second day in the Dodger dugout, Walt spoke briefly with Sandy Koufax as the Dodgers beat the Yankees again 4 to 1. Koufax was a native of Brooklyn and originally started with the Brooklyn Dodgers in 1955. He had friends and relatives in the Bronx, and they spoke about where the best Jewish Delis were located in the Bronx, Manhattan, and Brooklyn. Koufax took notes for the Bronx, while Walt took notes for Brooklyn in case he was assigned there in the future and needed a good pastrami sandwich with a kosher pickle and latka to go!

The teams left New York and on to Los Angeles, where the Yankees were swept in four games. A rarity for this powerful baseball team, but Walt could care less. He begrudgingly admitted he enjoyed speaking with the players but only on his terms..., no baseball questions. Furthermore, since Walt did not put up resistance to Captain Storm's assignment, he was rewarded in 1964 by being assigned the parking lot detail during the World Series with the St. Louis Cardinals. A win-win for everyone, except once again, the New York Yankees, who lost in seven to the St. Louis Cardinals.

Going into 1964 was a pivotal year for Walt. He became 40 years old and by year's end lost his father due to a heart attack. We all sensed Walt was changing, including his mother, May. However, life was changing drastically for her as well. She once again was visited by overwhelming premonitions, which foretold change but not for the better.

Chapter 22
Premonitions of Lou's Death in 1964

May was told by Lou and Walt not to utilize her "sixth sense", as this was a curse, not a blessing. However, after Lou died and May lived alone, both Roots and I visited her in her apartment in New York. We enjoyed this, as she liked our company, and we liked the haven away from Walt and June, and May had candy and spare coins she would press into our hands when we left her place, with the instructions to buy something nice, "but don't tell your father."

She told us stories we mostly forgot, but the one she repeated often, and that I therefore remember, is about the three warnings.

In 1964, May's husband, Lou, was 69 years old and happy with his two grandchildren and the fact that he financed a small two-bedroom, one-bath summer chalet at Lake Copake. He missed managing the post office station in the Bronx and missed his day-to-day interaction with his workmates, employees, and superiors. He was very well-liked for being a hard but fair worker. However,

Lou did smoke, overeat, and had hypertension. He even volunteered to work at a gasoline station, pumping gas and cleaning windshields just for tips. He loved to work and enjoyed talking to people.

In September 1964, we were closing down and winterizing the chalet for the winter. Roots and I were going back to school, and we would go up to the lake one or two more weekends to cut off water, winterize our small fishing boat, and generally get ready to say goodbye until late spring the next year.

We spent a forgettable weekend in the house, but Lou was not the same; he complained about heartburn and was very pale. We found out in less than two weeks that he had a heart attack and subsequently died. However, May told this story.

About three weeks before Lou died, they were in bed in New York City, when May heard Lou get up and go to the bathroom. He did not put on the light and partially closed the door. She heard things moving around in the medicine cabinet, and she got a little worried. She whispered, "Lou, are you alright?" No answer, so she spoke again louder and said, "Lou, what's wrong?" With that, a hand touched her, and Lou was right next to her and said, "What are you shouting about; I am right here." She was scared thinking there was an intruder, so Lou got up, turned the lights on, but no one was there. In his blunt Italian-American way he said, "It was nothing; you were just hearing things."

A few days later, Lou woke up at 7 am and went to the bathroom to shave. May was just getting out of bed and saw Lou's back to her but did not see his face or body in the reflection in the mirror. This startled her and she approached Lou, but as she got closer, the reflection returned as normal. At this time, she knew some bad news was coming and it would be about Lou.

The night before they left for Lake Copake together, May had a vivid bad dream where her husband Lou was calling her on the phone and said he was lost and afraid and couldn't find his way home. In the dream, May cried and said she would stay on the phone and guide him home. However, his voice became faint, and she cried and cried. May was awakened by Lou, who told her it was just a bad dream. She hugged him and said she feared the worst but Lou firmly said, "I don't believe in that bullshit, and neither should you. Let's go to the lake and see the grandchildren and forget this nonsense."

Upon spending the weekend in Lake Copake, Lou had heartburn and at the end, chest pains. He drove back to New York City and saw his doctor, who admitted him to the hospital. He died three days later.

Walt tended to ignore or downplay what May said, but I could see in his face he believed she experienced something. May always wondered out loud, "Why did the good Lord tell me this if there was nothing I could do to prevent his death?" Her Jewish friend, who was her age and lived next door, said, "Perhaps the signs were to allow you spiritually to prepare for his passing?"

I always wondered what May could have done with her "gift" if she would have developed it. However, with Lou and Walt, that would have been most difficult to do.

I wonder if I have some of her "magic" in my blood? What about my children? I can only say I hope so.

Walt ended 1964 with a bang and not a whimper, as described in the next chapter.

Chapter 23

A New Year's Eve Ambush

It was approaching New Year's Eve of 1964. Walt lucked out by getting the 4 pm to midnight shift, as the New Year's parties tend to go on all night, and around 4 to 5 am, trouble starts as drunks stagger out from bars, restaurants, and private residences looking for something to do during the first few hours of the New Year. While most people could hold their liquor and get home in one piece, others channelled their dark side and practised a little vandalism, or if feeling invincible, looked for a fight. Funnily enough, many people who are mild-mannered before drinks often turn into "Jekyll and Hyde" after getting drunk. He saw that even with his colleagues at the 46th Precinct.

The patrol cars pulled in at 11:30 pm to the station, and Walt went to his locker and changed into his civilian clothing. He put his trusted .38 Police Special with a long barrel into the locker and strapped on his .38 snub nose Special onto his belt. Walt always carried a gun in the City of New York along with his badge, even off duty. "You never know when your life will depend on it," he would say to anyone who was listening. Some of his partners asked if he wanted to bring in the New Year at Murphy's Bar just off the Grand Concourse. Walt declined, as he rarely drank and didn't like the company of drunks. He would always say, "You can never reason with a drunk in an argument. You have to deck them or walk away." He wanted to get home as the temperatures plunged, making the roads icy; and it will be twice as dangerous with icy roads and drunk drivers.

Earlier that day, Walt could only find parking six blocks from the station. While he was fortunate to have his rubber galoshes, he didn't think he would need his boots, and he left them in the locker. As he left the warmth of the station, he felt the bitter cold and slipped for the first time on the icy sidewalk. People getting in and out of cars were having a tough time keeping their balance. Walt counted the fifth block, which was on a slight hill, and he remembered how it took a great deal of effort to parallel park with limited space, on a hill, and with snow and ice to boot. "Maybe retiring to Florida would not be a bad idea," he thought as he slipped, skidded, and saw his new Oldsmobile Racing Green Cutlass only halfway down the block. "It will be warm and comfy," he thought with a smile. "I will be home in 25 minutes and in bed while the City goes crazy on New Year's Eve."

He was startled by a group of individuals who were exiting a private residence, already feeling no pain, and congregating in front of the building. There were four men and four women; the women with high heels and the men were planning to escort them to nearby cars. As Walt tried to pass, he slipped and unintentionally bumped one of the women. Walt said, "Sorry," and kept walking. With that, one of the men said, "Come back here and give the lady a proper apology, you fucking drunk." Walt turned to see all eight of them silent now and staring at him. He turned and continued to walk toward his car. "They are drunk and not worth arguing with," he thought. The man closest to Walt lunged and grabbed him by the lapel, sending Walt's fedora onto the ice. Walt quickly knocked the man's hands off of him and pushed him away and the man fell to the ground and struggled to get up.

With that, the other three men approached Walt with clenched fists. Under the streetlamp, they looked youngish, in their early twenties, clean-cut and did not fit Walt's internal profile for being thugs. The ringleader called Walt a "fucking drunk who will get his ass kicked now" and threw a punch which grased Walt's chin, but it stung as the fist was hard and the wind was cold. Walt swung at him, making a medium connection but almost fell to the ground due to the ice and the momentum of his body. A third guy tried to tackle him, but he too slipped and Walt was able to redirect him headfirst into a parked car.

The ringleader, the shortest of the group, about five feet 10 and 170 pounds said, "Get him, men. Knock him to the ground and kick his head in." Walt slowly managed to back himself toward the building to stop the men from attacking from behind. He was restricted in punching by his overcoat. Equally, as he was occasionally taking kicks and punches, the overcoat deflected the impact of these hits. Walt did notice that in his many fights, these guys were strong and they seemed to take orders from the ringleader. In a brief hiatus of the fight, Walt told them that he was an off-duty police officer, and they could now consider themselves under arrest. The ringleader said, "Fuck You!" The attacks on Walt continued, which seemed for hours in this bad situation. Walt tried to focus his punches on the ringleader in the hope that he would decide to withdraw. However, this did not happen. Each punch Walt landed seemed to escalate the fury of the attack even more.

The women at first tried to calm the men down, but Walt's comments about arresting them agitated them, and they started to go at him swinging purses at his head, or diving at him with their fingernails hoping to connect with his eyes.

Walt acknowledged to himself that he was in a tricky situation, in that he was now exhausted, and he was taking hits to the face and head three times for everyone he connected with. His only hope was that with all the commotion, somebody within the apartments would call the police. He also knew that under no circumstances, he should let them knock him down. He felt they were both so angry and drunk, that there would be a good chance of being kicked to death. He conserved his energy to block or redirect punches, trying to avoid getting kicked in the groin, but feeling the kicks hit the upper thigh. He got fewer and fewer punches in, as the belligerents moved closer and closer to land their punches and try to make him fall. Fortunately, the ice worked to Walt's advantage, and whenever they moved too quickly, both men and women landed on their asses, which enraged them even more.

It seemed like hours but it was less than 10 minutes when a police car from the 46th Precinct arrived and Walt's two partners, John Clarke and Ken Steed came and quickly brought an end to the fight with two of the fighters, including the ringleader taking a wrap over the head with nightsticks. Clarke and Steed were surprised to see Walt and joked that, "Now we know this was the real party you wanted to go to." Walt was barely conscious and an ambulance took him to Fordham Hospital for treatment.

The fighters and their girlfriends were booked for felonious assault on a police officer, drunk and disorderly behavior, and concealed weapon, as one of the men carried a switchblade. Steed thought the cop fighters would get at least three years in prison, and the women would probably get away with a year suspended sentence. They will all have a felony record and can kiss their futures goodbye. Walt smiled but said he couldn't laugh as his jaw and ribs hurt too much. But admittedly, the thought of this cheered him up.

Around 7 am on New Year's Day, an Inspector, Robert Hearn, visited Walt. Hearn was in his formal blue uniform with the gold braiding, and his police guard and escort accompanied him. "How are you feeling?" he asked with an Irish brogue and seemed really concerned. Walt told him that he would live but hoped the police dental plan would pay for the dental work, as he lost a couple of teeth and had a minor concussion. Inspector Hearn told Walt, "We take care, good care of our own; don't worry about medical or dental bills." Walt smelt a rat, and said he was honored to be visited by an inspector, but usually, an inspector would only visit if the policeman had a gunshot wound. Why the high ranking visit?

Hearn smiled sheepishly and said that the party Walt and his partners arrested were well connected. He said the four men are seniors at the United States Military Academy at West Point and will graduate next June. The girls attend university at private girl schools, and their fathers would appreciate it if Walt dropped the charges. Walt protested, "They were drunk, violent and could have killed me, inspector." "They are merely children letting off steam," said Hearn. "Do they need to be punished? Of course, and their parents will deal with them, but remember that two US Senators and two Congressmen nominated those normally outstanding men to the military academy. They need to graduate, and the girls need to go back to school; they can not do this with a criminal record. Besides, those four assholes will probably go to Vietnam and get wasted or fragged over there." Hearn stopped smiling and looked at Walt seriously and said, "Officer, do you understand?" Walt hated himself for this but nodded in the affirmative. Inspector Hearn put his hand on Walts's shoulder and said, "Good. Everything works out in the end. You are doing the right thing, officer." Hearn left the hospital room and Walt never saw him again.

A police courier came by within an hour with completed paperwork, which stated everything was a misunderstanding; the parties involved were embarrassed by what happened and Walt accepted their apologies. Walt had an offer he couldn't refuse and, loathing himself, signed the document and dropped charges against all eight individuals.

He finally got home to celebrate New Year's Day with his family. He told Roots and me what happened, and said the bruises hurt, but the documents he signed hurt a lot more. It took me years to understand what he meant. Nothing is as it seems, and there wasn't equal justice for all, there was "just us" who seemed to be protected.

Walt recovered from the assault and started to seriously think about retiring from the police force and moving away from New York City; however, where to move was a critical question, and he said we needed to take more road trips to find a new home. A period of family vacations started to the chagrin of Roots and me.

Chapter 24

A Holiday from a Holiday

While staying in the Lake Copake chalet, Walt would get tired of his holiday there and want to take a holiday from his holiday. One evening, in 1966, he told Roots and me that he wanted to take us to Quebec City, Canada, for a short holiday. We protested, as we had made a few friends with some of the vacationing children. They owned a beautiful collie called Rusty, and we enjoyed playing with the dog and tolerated its owners. However, Walt insisted that we would have fun and prepare for a 10-hour road trip to Canada. While I was curious to visit a foreign country, and this predated by two years our family vacation to California, we only mildly resisted. As expected, our resistance was stopped by being called "two ungrateful pieces of shit" by Walt, and June crying and saying, "Did you really have to call them that?" Walt shouted back and said, "Yes, I could call these little fuckers something far worse." A good time was guaranteed for all!

The long and tedious trip was almost unremarkable with the standard cigarette smoke in the car with windows closed, Roots sitting and sleeping in the back of the car with June, trying to avoid the smoke. I sat in the front as a navigator and was told to pay attention and not miss various turnoff points. Long, tedious, and boring was the name of the game until we reached the US-Canadian border. At the border crossing, Walt produced his New York driver's license and was asked why we were going to Canada. His response was, "To eat smoked salmon, French pastry, and drink the delicious beer." Everyone laughed and before I knew it, we were in my first foreign country. At first glance, the scenery was the same as upstate New York, but I was thrilled to see that the signs of the towns and villages were in French. Also, I saw that the churches had longer and higher steeples. There was a difference and I thought this could be somewhat interesting. Walt turned on the AM radio and we listened to French news, which no one could understand, and French music, which was alright.

It was still a long haul from the border to Quebec, and this leg of the drive seemed to take forever as well. We had reservations at a small inn just on the outskirts of the city. It was an older building, and the furnishing was adequate but seemed to be lots of browns and darker colors. Walt said, "So, what do you think of the place?" I said in a neutral tone, "Alright." June said it looked depressing," and Roots said, "I want to go home." Walt erupted with, "You fucking ingrates; I drove you 12 hours, and is this the shit I am going to get?" June sparked up a bit and said it was alright and said she saw swings in the front of the building for Roots and me to play on. Walt decompressed a little and, thankfully, that was all to that outburst.

Outside, Roots and I played on the swings but were soon approached by two Canadian children, a boy roughly my age and a girl Roots age. They only spoke in French but seemed to want to play. Walt was there and we asked him if he spoke French. Walt said he remembered a few words from high school and told me something phonetically to say. I said what I thought Walt told me and the boy punched me on the shoulder; he took his little sister by the hand and went into the house and slammed the door. We wondered what that was about but Walt looked perplexed and said maybe he got the words or pronunciation wrong. Roots and I decided to do our best not to try Walt's French for the rest of the trip.

We drove to a small restaurant that served fresh water trout and assorted local delicacies, which we all enjoyed. When we ordered, Walt insisted on speaking in French. The waitress frowned and said in accented English, "Please order in English, as I cannot understand your French." We all had a chuckle as Walt just successfully managed his temper.

On the menu, they told a story about a waterfall nearby and a "Woman in White," who tragically died there many years ago. Her ghost is reportedly seen. I asked Walt if we could look for this "Lady in White," as she seemed cool. Walt said, "If you want to see ghosts, we will go to the Plains of Abraham after dinner, as it was an important battlefield that must have ghosts." It sounded like a plan, and we arrived at the Plains of Abraham around 10 pm.

Roots was totally freaked out, as he didn't like the sound of ghosts, and June said she would stay in the car with him. Walt and I started our nocturnal stroll over the landscape, which coincidentally offered a great night time view over Quebec City. It was a little creepy wondering if something would spring out at us like in most TV shows in the 1960s. There was nothing like that. However, I was looking at the fort, where General Montcalm of France unsuccessfully tried to hold off Major General Wolfe of Great Britain, when I thought I saw a flash of fire and smoke come out of the opening of a cannon overlooking the battlefield. I yelled to Walt, "Dad, did you see that?" Walt said, "No; describe what you saw." He listened but said it was probably a reflection of a car's light. I said, "Do car lights smoke?" He told me, "Don't be a fresh mouth," and we walked back to the car. As we were almost in the car, June and Roots were pointing towards something in the middle of the field. We turned and looked, and about 30 feet away I saw the shape of a man in uniform, which gave off a dull glow. The head was weird as it slowly marched generally in our direction; it seemed that the figure was missing the upper part of its head, from the nose up. This scared the living daylights out of me, and I know Walt saw it too, as he said, "Get in the car. We are going now." I had an uncomfortable feeling walking around that battlefield. For me, this experience was my first introduction to the paranormal, and it was definitely scary.

Once we were in the car, Walt downplayed what we saw. Was it because he didn't expect to really see anything, and this was not planned? June and Roots insisted it was real, but Walt told us all to shut up, or we would give ourselves nightmares. We arrived back at the hotel and slept without nightmares, except we had to do the museum circuit the next day. This was truly tedious, and we remember seeing displays of French missionaries being tortured to death by Native Americans, and what seemed to be hundreds of oil on canvas paintings of long-dead generals and governors of Quebec. Roots and I longed to get back to the lake and see our friends.

The last memorable thing that occurred is that Roots and I badgered Walt to buy some fireworks, as they were legal in Canada but illegal, or just not sold, in New York. Walt bought an assortment of fireworks in a large box, but a few miles from the border, he had second thoughts. What if these were confiscated at the border as contraband? We pulled over, as Walt had a plan.

June sat in the back with Roots lying and sleeping on top of the fireworks covered in a blanket. "What if they ask us to get out of the car, Dad?" I asked. "We go to Plan B," he said, "I go to jail and your mother, brother and you get jobs." He smiled, but I worried. Roots got into sleeping mode, and even his breathing made us all feel sleepy.

At the border, the US Customs Officer asked if we bought anything to declare, and we showed him a bag of Canadian flag pennants for our bedroom and picture books of Quebec. He looked in at Roots and said, "I wish I could sleep as well as he can." He chuckled and waved us through the border. We made it!

The postscript is that we enjoyed the fireworks back at Lake Copake during the Fourth of July that year. The road trip, while tedious and boring, was acceptable, and we took home a ghost story which still makes us wonder what really happened on the Plains of Abraham that night in 1966.

Chapter 25

A Visit to the 1967 New York City Boat Show

Walt liked boats, cars, and airplanes - we have established this; and he enjoyed going Downtown to the Coliseum to go to the Boat Show. In 1967, he asked, "Do you want to come with me?" and I said, "Yes." This meant I could ride the subway, which I loved. Walt preferred the express bus but agreed to take a taxi to the end of the line. We entered a dark subway station to begin the journey. Back then, I felt invincible, as Walt had a snub nose Special, a badge, and he even carried handcuffs - just in case.

As we entered the station, a tall thin 55-year-old black man with an unkempt greyish white beard approached us and said, "Excuse me, sir, I am not begging, but could you lend me a dollar for...." Walt cut in with a harsh voice and said, "Beat it, you fucking skell." The man politely said, "Yes, sir" and disappeared into the shadows.

We boarded the front car, and I kept my eyes peeled for any ghosts, monsters, or fiends lurking in the dark tunnels ahead of us. As we approached stations, I became disappointed but still loved the thrill of entering the tunnels for another chance to witness the otherworld of the supernatural. We never did see anything remotely spooky, but I felt we accomplished a lot as a nine-year-old boy when we arrived at the Coliseum.

Inside we viewed all types of boats, but Walt focused on pleasure craft, which was staged usually with enticing scenery for photographs and inspection. I remember taking a picture of me holding a cardboard marlin, which, in reflection, made me look like I was in Florida deep sea fishing with my overcoat on! I still have this photo.

I started to get excited, as Walt spoke with different salesmen and asked for brochures and said the various boats looked "just right for us." We had a small chalet in upstate New York that Walt's father bought for us before his passing away in 1964. We had a large dock, the second largest on the lake at the time. I mistakenly thought we were going to get a cool motorboat to moor next to the cool dock, but as the night wore on, I got the feeling this was not on the table, as every conversation was the same and we built up a thick stack of brochures and that was about it.

Roots and I learned in later life that this was a very frustrating Walt tactic of obtaining live entertainment from boat, aircraft, and car salesmen without ever buying anything. He was just looking for something to do.

As the show was getting ready to end, we went to the nearby restaurant, Horn & Hardart Automat, for dinner. What is an Automat? Well, it was the coolest restaurant on earth, in my opinion, in 1967. Behind hundreds of small glass doors, you could look at a variety of sandwiches, and if you liked one, you would put coins into a receptacle; the glass door would open and you would collect your sandwich on a white china plate. I never understood how Walt would opt for the hot roast beef sandwich with mash potatoes and gravy on the cafeteria line, as I wanted to use the automat machine. After my cold sandwich and Walt's hot sandwich, we both ordered a slice of apple pie with a slice of cheddar cheese on top. I was thrilled that I could put the coins in and take the pie out of the glass doors. I still wonder if this was because of the taste of the food, the fun of operating the automat, or having dinner with Dad? It certainly was memorable.

I had hoped to get a subway back to the Bronx, but it was approaching 11 pm that night, and Walt said, "We will take the express bus home, as I just don't want to deal with these fucking degenerates, scumbags, and skells." This was my cue not to argue but just be grateful for the night out without incident.

My night was complete and the next morning told Roots about what happened. He said he was glad I had a good time, but he also had a good time eating bacon, toast, and grape jelly, plus chocolate milk, and he too was not yelled at or whacked. A win-win for both of us.

After the summer of 1967, Walt put the Lake Copake chalet up for sale. Roots and I were sad at first but were told in 1968 that we would go to Disneyland instead.

This was an acceptable exchange, until we found out it wasn't a trip by airline but by car. The dreaded family vacation.

Chapter 26

Walt's Road Trip to California

In June 1968, Walt decided to take the wife and two boys on a family vacation. This was not at all dissimilar to Chevy Chase's film, Family Vacation. Where to start? How about the beginning.

The purpose of the epic drive from New York City to Anaheim, California, was to visit Disneyland and to look for possible retirement homes for Walt after he retired from the NYPD. The night before the journey, Walt and June made a dozen or more tuna fish, ham and cheese, egg mayonnaise, and salami sandwiches. The idea was to leave the apartment at 5 am and beat the traffic on the first leg of our trip to California. We planned to get there in 5 days if Walt could keep up the pace. After we pulled out of the parking lot, Walt wanted a sandwich. As we drove to the Henry Hudson Parkway, about three minutes from home, Walt wanted another sandwich. In the meantime, June lit up a cigarette, and the windows were closed for the entire trip. The maggot-gagging smell of cigarette smoke, tuna fish, and egg mayonnaise with the stench of an occasional stale fart, clung to the car as we crossed the George Washington Bridge.

By the time we were in New Jersey around 5:30 am, the sandwiches were gone! My brother Roots had his head stuck under a blanket, trying desperately to filter the stench that permeated within the car in his hopeless search for stench-free air. We were off and all was good, until we reached the Pennsylvania Turnpike and traveled west toward Ohio.

We started to notice the car, a brand new Oldsmobile Delta 88, started to sputter. At first, every few minutes, but as we religiously ignored the problem, the sputtering continued, until it became apparent after passing the last exit ramp, and the next one was 14 miles away, that we were not going to make it. Walt pulled off to the side of the road as he cursed his bad luck, his bad mechanic, and General Motors. After fooling around looking cluelessly under the hood, a friendly State Trooper stopped and radioed for a tow truck.

We were towed to a gas station with a mechanic on duty, who looked at the car and said the carburetor was filthy. Walt's local mechanic, who charged 145 dollars to service the car from top to bottom, failed to change the filter. Walt was able to convince the mechanic to make the repairs, and in 4 hours. And for less than 275 dollars, we were back on the road. "My whole week's fucking salary spent, because that fucking scumbag in the Bronx fucked me over at Carlo's Car Repair." We heard this mantra or variations for this until we arrived late at our Holiday Inn in Indiana.

The road trip continued from Indiana to Missouri, when Walt noticed that the car was getting hard to control and we pulled over to the side again. "Fuck, we have a fucking flat!" Walt bellowed. As cars raced by us, Walt had to take out all the suitcases packed in the car's trunk and access the spare. He was able to change the tire, but now he had to repack the trunk and go to a garage to fix the flat.

At the garage, Walt was told that the tear in the tire was too big to fix, and now he had to spend another 100 dollars for a new tire. Walt was livid and cried out, "If one more thing happens to us, we are selling this fucking car and flying back to New York." Roots, who was missing his friends, said, "Good." While Walt was now on the highway, driving 70 mph, and trying to turn around to hit Roots for agreeing with him. We swayed from one lane to another as Walt flayed Roots, who was all of 8 years old and hiding under a blanket and lying on the car floor. "You mealy-mouth piece of shit," Walt cried as, again, he tried to strike Roots with a firm punch. However, Roots saw the seriousness of the situation, as Walt kept swinging away, and started crying, which did the trick, and Walt continued driving on to California.

Next, in New Mexico, Walt wanted to stay in Santa Fe, and we pulled into an old historic hotel. This structure with some Art Deco Spanish architecture loomed in Santa Fe, just daring us to come in. It may have been a showcase in the 1920s and 1930s, but Roots and I sensed trouble as we entered. This super-sucked, as unlike the Holiday Inn, it had no swimming pool and no air conditioner. As June was a chain smoker, and we were at a high altitude, she lay on the floor of the hotel room trying to breathe. I noticed a mouse on the floor and mentioned it to June, and I got a smack in the face for my trouble. "You fucking sadistic bastard," said Walt. I cried, while June gasped for air, Roots hid under his blanket, and Walt swore as loud as he could for all our unfortunate neighbors in that hothouse hotel to hear our fucking angst.

The next morning, I convinced Walt to buy some fireworks, as what boy did not like fireworks? They were for sale along the road in New Mexico. Walt relented, but we could only buy miniature firecrackers, as real firecrackers will "blow your fucking hand clear off," lectured Walt. We bought tiny little crackers and then, at the next rest stop, wanted to shoot them off. Again Walt relented and took the fireworks from us and climbed up a slight mound, and with his cigarette, he lit a miniature firecracker. He ran down the hill like a bat out of hell and proceeded to stumble. He rolled down the hill, hit the bottom, and then we heard just a faint "pop," where the firecracker exploded. We needed to drive to the hospital to have Walt's arm mended. I asked Walt if he needed to run away from such a small firecracker, and I got a wrap in the mouth for being a smart ass.

After visiting the hospital and getting Walt's arm X-rayed and bandaged for a bad sprain, we continued our quest for nirvana. This led us to Las Vegas and our newest adventure.

On Frontier Street, Walt took us to a casino, The Golden Nugget. Roots and I were thrilled with the idea of playing slots, and Walt, an active New York City policeman, gave Roots (age 8) and me (age 10) a 20-dollar bill and told us to ask the friendly policeman inside the casino where we could get some change. We unknowingly obeyed Walt, and when we spoke to the policeman inside the casino, he wanted to know where our parents were. We took him to Walt, and he gave Walt a tongue lashing about how stupid and illegal it was to take children into a casino. Walt diplomatically said he was sorry and took us to another casino but made us stand outside and point to the machines we wanted him to play.

Next, we visited Lake Havasu, Arizona. This seemed very close to hell on earth, as the temperature pushed to 120 F. Walt, however, wanted to look at real estate. We went to an on-duty agent who asked what he wanted. Walt said, "At least twenty acres, away from people, quiet, and on a slight elevation." The agent said he had something, and Walt added "at 200 dollars per acre." "This is difficult, Walt, but I still can find what you want," the agent said with a smile.

We drove with the agent for what seemed like an eternity, though it was probably only 15 minutes. But the windows were down, and we were roasting alive in the back of his car. Next, he stopped and said, "Everything you want, Walt; 22 acres, elevated, on an access road, also access to water, very important in Arizona. All for 200 dollars per acre." Walt shook his head and said, "Where are the hospitals, the doctor's offices, the police, the schools, universities, the restaurants, the cinemas, and the airport?" The agent scratched his head and said, " Walt, you do not want to live in the country, you want to live in the heart of New York City on 20 acres at 200 dollars per acre." He added, "I feel like you have been jerking me off." Walt knew in his heart that the guy was right and made an excuse to leave town fast.

But not so fast. As we were leaving Lake Havasu, Walt had another flat, different tire, previously inspected by his buddy, Carlos. Now with one arm in the sling, Walt cursed the universe, the stars, and the fact he was born, unloaded the trunk, took out the spare, changed the tire with one arm, reloaded the trunk, and we drove off into the loving embrace of Death Valley. Once again, Roots asked Walt if we would sell the car and go home, and once again, he took a smack in the face. A cry, a curse, a sigh from June, and I asked why, as we headed off into the sunset.

The next stop was California.

In the tedious drive to California, there was constant bickering, cursing, and whacks in the face. However, in the desert, we stopped at a gas station. Roots and I talked Walt into buying a strange-looking cannonball souvenir for 50 cents. In reality, it was a geode that was found in the area but looked cool. The man at the counter said he was a Native American, and if the center of the geode had the image of an owl, this would be worth 25,000 dollars. However, to cut it open, he wanted another 50 cents. Roots and I turned to Walt and said, "Please, let's do it." Walt said, as if the man was not present, "No, if they do find something, this fucking jerk-off will say it was his all along and we will get nothing." With that, we left the gas station/souvenir shop with the man shaking his head in amazement.

Once we arrived near Los Angeles, Walt constantly took wrong turns, spinning us off to unknown suburbs far from our target, Anaheim. This caused Walt to go into tirades that even we hadn't heard before. His main target, other than Californians in general, were the makers of his maps, Rand McNally, who Walt said was a company that was "spawn of Satan" for making the maps incomprehensible, especially to Walt. However, despite the fun of the divergences, we finally made it to Anaheim. Tomorrow is Disney and this sets us up for the next adventure.

We were relieved to get to Disney. The next day, a friendly young Southern Californian man, around 21 years old, by the name of Danny, took us by golf cart from our motel across the street to the entrance of the park. Danny, in hindsight, was probably working for tips and Walt was not really in a generous mood. When we arrived at the entrance, Danny said with a big smile, "Hey guys, I play Happy and Grumpy of the Seven Dwarfs as an actor inside Disneyland on weekends; do you want my autograph?" Walt then yelled, "Hey guys, let's move it while the line is short and leave this fucking creep alone." Danny looked dejected as we ran off to enjoy the day.

At Disney, as we were closing in on the flagship ride, Pirates of the Caribbean, Walt and June stopped us and pointed out an elegant man, with nicely combed grey hair, in a suit and tie. He was too well dressed for the other people in the park, and he was not towing children or grandchildren. I asked if it was Walt Disney and Walt replied, "Disney died a couple of years ago, asshole." June said it was Joe DiMaggio, formerly of the New York Yankees and ex-husband to Marilyn Monroe. "Go ask for his autograph," Walt instructed.

Roots and I nervously approached Joe, but he seemed actually relieved that he was recognized and happily signed autographs for the two of us. He asked us where we were from, and we said New York City. He said, "Which team is your favorite - Yankees, or Mets? We said, "Yankees," and he broke into a big signature grin and said, "Good." Later on, we heard Joe stopped signing autographs unless he was paid 300 dollars per signature. We both still have his autograph in our personal collections.

After two days of Disneyland, Roots and I wanted to stay there forever, but we had to go to Hollywood to go on a backlot tour. We remembered it was hot, it sucked, and we were always thirsty and complaining, and got smacked accordingly. Our final destination was Knott's Berry Farm, where we remember panning for gold, and we still have a little gold dust from the day. However, when one of the hosts asked Walt if he was enjoying his stay, and what he thought of the place, Walt replied, "It's a poor man's Disney, and we won't be coming back." I am sure this really upset them.

On the drive back to New York, we took a more southern route and visited Tombstone, Arizona. While the idea of the Old Wild West still appeals to me, our memory of the place was that it was hot, dusty, little to no air conditioning, and the shootouts were hard to see, as the sweat got into our eyes along with the hot and relentless sun. Also, Walt didn't like the fucking creeps (reenactors) always begging for money.

Prior to leaving Arizona, Walt wanted us to go to Mexico and drive on the Mexican side of the border. I first thought this sounded cool but found out otherwise. The town of Nogales, in 1968, looked unfriendly and appeared unkempt. Roots and I were dying for a drink, and Walt yelled, "June, don't let them drink the water, or they will die of a parasite." He bought us a Coke, which we guzzled, and then we asked him if we could buy a souvenir, and he said, "No; it is all shit here. We have to go inside Mexico proper to find the good stuff." We drove and drove, and at one point, we got lost and traveled up a mountain that at the time seemed the size of Everest, and I remember looking out the window and seeing no barrier or fence, just a drop into infinity and beyond. I just closed my eyes and prayed we would get back safely to Arizona, which we eventually did.

The rest of the journey through Brownsville, Texas, was mostly unmemorable. Walt had to take us to where he was stationed during World War II, which in 1968 was a hot and unremarkable town. He took us to the beach, which he said he used to visit in 1944, and asked us if we would like to live here. We said no, it was hot and we missed our friends in New York. This qualified for a smack in the face for being "a fresh mouth."

The rest of the trip was alright, or at least we do not remember any major breakdowns, fights, or unwanted commotion. We eventually made it to Clearwater, Florida, where our grandparents lived. Roots and I complained to Granddad, who smiled and said, "Guess you will always remember this adventure." He got that right. While being in a small house with our grandparents sounds boring, it was much better than being cooped up in a car for 10 hours a day. We had access to a pool, shuffleboard, and an occasional friend. We were happy the trip came to an end.

Did we enjoy Disney? Yes, but would we want to do this all again with Walt and June?

Walt finally decided we would move to Florida, as the property and taxes were too high in California, and things were too hot in Arizona and Texas. June had her parents in Florida and we, therefore, had a platform when we resettled there.

Walt said he wanted to leave the police department but told the following story that happened just before retirement.

Chapter 27

A Bloody Sunday in the Bronx

It was a crisp late spring morning in the 46th Precinct with Walt and his long time partner of almost ten years, John Nester, cruising down East Gun Hill Road in the Bronx. They just feasted on a plain donut and a hot black coffee each. Both men wanted another donut, yet in their hearts knew that the tightening waistline of their uniform trousers was not due to the coffee, but to the donut, and occasionally the second was somewhat a less delicious follow-up to the first.

It seemed as if it would be a relatively quiet morning, as only a handful of people were out and about at 9:15 am. Only a couple of coffee shops selling bagels and cream cheese were open, as the area was changing. The unique "Jewishness" of the area was becoming more Hispanic and more African-American. The old shops were closing, being replaced by different foods, clothing, and styles. Additionally, crime was increasing, and there were more and more arrests being made from Friday evening to Sunday morning. But this Sunday seemed calm.

Ahead, from the police cruiser, Walt and John saw a small group of well-dressed women filing out from a nearby Baptist Church. In the past, there were mostly synagogues with only the occasional Catholic or Lutheran Churches, but things were changing. At least a block away, one woman, walking slower and behind the others, limped forward. She too, was dressed in her Sunday best with a hat and a large handbag, with her hand firmly around the leather straps. They could see that this woman, like the others, was black and seemed elderly by the way she moved. Just then, darting around the corner, was a young man, also black but dressed in jeans, sweatshirt, and sneakers. Almost like out of a film, in no time, he identified the lone woman and yanked at her handbag, which she amazingly held on to. The woman fell to the sidewalk, landing squarely on her rear end, but maintaining control of her precious bag. With that, the mugger kicked the old woman, as hard as he possibly could, and she recoiled backward, her head slamming to the concrete ground, and she let go of the bag. The assailant hesitated a moment, but at that very second, Walt turned on the siren and lights and said to Nester, "Whatever we do, let's catch that fucking scumbag." The mugger jumped, as he was startled at the magical appearance of the police car he had not seen just before the attack. He dropped the handbag and ran like a greyhound toward an alley, which had chain-linked fences with adjacent car repair and storage facilities.

In a matter of seconds, Walt barked an order to Nester to get him, while he radioed an ambulance. The other women in front of the older injured lady came back to assist, as Walt told the dispatcher that a woman had severe head injuries, and an ambulance was needed urgently. Walt was burning with rage, as he thought of his mother, who just as easily could have been targeted for a similar senseless attack. He asked the ladies to stay and wait with the injured woman for an ambulance, as he felt the need to help his partner find the soulless scumbag who committed this crime.

As Walt was speaking to the women, who were shocked, saddened, but trying to help, he heard the frail woman on the ground say, "Officer, please come here." He was just moving in the direction of the alley but the tone and sweetness of the voice made him pause. "Please, officer, I need you," she said. Walt went to her and kneeled down to both listen to her and examine her wounds up close. She was a bloody mess. She was bleeding from the back of the head, where it hit the sidewalk, and from her nose and mouth, where the young assailant kicked her in the face. The old woman was at least 75 years old, but maybe older. She was shaken, going in shock, yet kept command of the tone of her voice but struggled to keep awake. "Please hold my hand," she said. Walt knew two things, and both at that moment, as he grasped her hand; it was as certain as the sun would come up every morning. One was that he would not have the pleasure of helping his partner catch the mugger, as too much time has passed. The second was that he somehow knew this woman would die. How, he wasn't sure, as in the distance he heard the siren of the ambulance, but this made no difference; he knew all the same.

The old woman struggled to look at Walt, and he took his handkerchief and placed it under her head, so at least there would be some cushion for her. He wiped the blood from her eyes and spoke words that he really did not believe, like, "You will be alright, just hang on Momma."

The woman's and Walt's roles momentarily changed, as he felt she sensed his grief and tried to somehow cheer him up with a stoic smile. Finally, she said, "Officer, how fortunate I am to have a handsome policeman act as my honor guard as I transition from this world to the next. Be in peace and thank you for staying with me to the end." She smiled reassuringly at Walt, and she closed her eyes and died. Just then, the emergency crew arrived; they put her in the back of the ambulance, and Walt later heard she was pronounced dead at Montefiore Hospital at 10:10 am.

The young man who did this was a boy; sixteen years old. He needed money to take his new girlfriend out and did not mean to hurt the woman. He was charged with second-degree murder, but this was plea-bargained to manslaughter. He served two years in a juvenile detention center and was released just after his 18th birthday.

The family who lost a mother and grandmother suffered the most. She had helped put her sons through school and was planning to help her grandchildren as well, through her pension from the social security bureau where she worked and retired.

Walt and John Nester attended the funeral of Gladys Jones, age 78, as they wanted to meet and see the family who had such a delightful matriarch. Walt told the woman's sons what happened in the end, and they each hugged both Walt and Nester. Walt later admitted he secretly shed a tear when Gladys died. This is the only work-related instance he ever admitted to me.

This was Walt's last police story and then he moved us to Florida, where we attempted to resettle. In retrospect, it was difficult for all of us, but it impacted Walt the hardest.

Chapter 28

Hoarding in Paradise

Walt did not transition well from the NYPD to Florida retirement. Let's face it, he never really transitioned, and despite everything he loathed about New York City and being a cop, he never got over the buzz of the streets. My brother and I saw it in his eyes and heard it in his voice; he missed the excitement, the power, and the control he thought that he held while a policeman.

The plan, in January 1971, was to retire with his police pension and live a happy life in West Florida near Tampa. Yeah right. The fun started almost immediately. First, you had economic issues; the US closed the gold counter to foreign governments, and the dollar was no longer, at least technically, supported by gold. Inflation hit hard and prices started rocketing up. We needed to spend less or eat into our limited savings. This troubled Walt.

Social unrest as the Vietnam War was starting to wind down slowly, and college and minority protests highlighted the unraveling of society as we knew it. This also bothered Walt.

Walt, if anything, was authoritarian, and he saw many things, and did not like most of them. He was complicated, as he expected people to obey authority, but he, however, did not think the rules applied to him. A funny thing happened when President Nixon asked the American people to support wage and price freezes and not to panic shop. Walt woke my brother and me up at 7 am the next morning, and we drove to a Lukens grocery store. There, he told us to fill the shopping cart with filet mignon, dozens of cans of Campbell's Soup (lots of tomato. Yuck), pork chops, chicken, and canned tuna fish. We were embarrassed, as the TV in the store was replaying the President's address to America about not hoarding, and here we were with more food than we could ever eat in a month, piling the hoard onto the counter. While most people were buying a quart of milk and a loaf of bread and some hamburger meat, we were hoarding! Walt did not find this amusing; he was serious!

If this seems funny, things got worse. Walt's mother, May, was in her late 70s and a fish out of water after being taken away from her friends in New York City, where she was self-sufficient. She was now forced to live with us in a suburban home with no access to stores, shops or friends unless Walt took her by car. She went insane and no one really knew why. No one really cared, as everyone was trying to adjust in their own way to Florida. She later graduated from moaning and crying to pissing, then shitting on the floors, and my brother and I had to maneuver around Grandma's piss, shit, and occasional vomit, as this was just a typical day. We all were desperately trying to find our own way in this hot, humid, bug-infested climate, where jobs paid minimum wage and schools were at very best below average. Oh, did I say our mom, June, started to drink heavily as menopause, heat, humidity, stress, and Walt broke her down? Mom would, according to Walt, not go to sleep but pass out due to alcohol abuse and depression.

We bought a dog, an Airedale, which helped somewhat, but he seemed to, at best, tolerate us but seemed to dislike Walt. Funny, Walt liked the dog, but even now, I remember how Walt, ramping up from anger to rage, would tell my brother and me that we were no good cocksuckers and we needed to get up early and weed the garden. Walt would get up at 7 am with my brother and I, when it was barely cool during Florida's long summers. I remember hearing Walt putting the chain leash around the 100-pound dog, who was mostly muscle, hair, and teeth, and whose name was Joey. We would hear, "Stay still, you fucking bastard!" and the dog would bark, as it was excited as it was going to the car. We then heard the dog piss on the croton plant by the entranceway, and the flow of urine made us want to piss as well.

Next, we would hear Walt open the squeaky door of his dilapidated 1964 Oldsmobile, which Granddad, June's father, had given to us out of pity, as Walt was unemployed and making ends meet on a fixed pension from the New York Police Department. Next, we would hear Walt try to start the car. It never turned over on the first or second tries. It sometimes needed three or more turns of the key, with the sound of this piece-of-shit car engine trying desperately to turn over. Meanwhile, Joey would be barking with the window open and Walt would be shouting in the early morning at the top of his lungs, "Shut up, you hairy bastard!" The car would finally choke into action and would go "putt, putt, putt" as Walt would back down the semi-circular driveway. Then, my brother and I would hear the clunking of the automatic transmission as Walt drove forward, with the dog barking and Walt cursing. My brother and I would start to go back to sleep as the barking, cursing, and clunking of the piece-of-shit car drove off to the nearby nature park where Joey would run and play.

My brother and I would have about 40-45 minutes of additional sleep before we would hear some noise in the distance - Joey barking, the clanging of the piece-of-shit car, and Walt cursing at the dog. As the Oldsmobile drove up the driveway, the car would grind to a halt. Walt would turn the car engine off, but it would continue to putt, cough, backfire, and finally give up the ghost and stop. We would then hear Walt open the rear door, which was loud and squeaky. He would then slam it shut and say, "Go into the house you fucking cocksucker." Presumably, this was to Joey who would take another piss on the plant outside the door. Walt would enter the house, slam the door, and yell, "Get up, you two bastards, and get to work on the lawn." My brother and I would look at each other and say, "Another Day in Paradise," but little did we know Walt was still only just ramping up.

Roots and I won a silent but big victory, when Walt lost a battle with the lawnmower repairman, which could be dubbed, "The Battle of the Lawn-Boy."

Chapter 29
Walt Confronted by the Lawnmowing Repairman

After arriving in Florida, a memorable story that occurred was Walt's battle with the "Lawn-Boy" lawnmower. Our ranch-style house had lots of grass, and in Florida, we have lots of rain and sun, and in the long summer, the lawn had to be cut at least once a week. While Granddad, June's father, suggested that we hire a lawn service, Walt said, "We have two boys who can earn their keep by mowing the lawn." My brother Roots and I ended up calling ourselves "Lawn Apes," as we would mow for almost two hours in the sun, with high humidity, and with the lawnmower throwing off dirt and grass, and we would literally be drenched in sweat with filth and grass clinging to us. We hated doing this every single week, as we stunk, were bitten by insects, and were dehydrated and exhausted after doing this.

As the work was hot and dirty, the lawnmower would kick this filth up into its motor and would break down. This would require us to lift the lawnmower, which was heavy, and put it into the car and take it to a lawnmower repair shop in a nearby town. Walt, being a Northerner, did not immediately see that his style did not fit the local Southern etiquette. For example, he entered the shop one day and said to the owner and repairman, Dan Quesenberry, who looked like he did and still could play professional football at a very well preserved age of 40, that the Lawn-Boy mower wasn't working.

Dan asked, "Why?"

"Somehow there is grass in the fuel tank."

"You should cut the grass and bag it, but don't put it in the tank." Dan was joking with a dry Southern sense of humor, which Walt did not quite understand nor appreciate.

"Well, just fix it."

"I would like to, but it will take at least two weeks."

"I need it next week."

"Then it will cost you extra."

"How much?" barked Walt.

"Well," Dan said slowly, "10 dollars for two weeks' wait, but 20 dollars for one week."

Walt was furious but had no choice and agreed to 20 dollars for the following week. Dan said, "OK, see you next Saturday but don't forget the 20 dollars."

On the drive home, Walt cursed Dan and said, "That rebel son-of-a-bitch thinks he got me over a barrel, but I will show him a thing or two." However, the following Saturday, we collected the Lawn-Boy and paid Dan his 20 dollars. Dan said, "Now, Walt, don't be putting any more grass into the gas tank, got it?" with the biggest shit-eating grin I ever saw. Walt turned red and stormed out. About three weeks later, the same thing happened again with virtually the same dialog. This time, however, Dan spoke kindly to myself and my brother and asked in front of Walt, "How do you put up with him?" We all laughed but Walt. After spending 40 dollars on repairs for a relatively new lawnmower, Walt concocted a failsafe plan.

In two weeks, the mower had the same problem, but what Walt did was drive down the block from Dan's Lawn Mowers and Repairs, and we took the Lawn-Boy out of the trunk and pushed it to Dan's shop. Walt stayed in the air-conditioned car, and Roots and I met up with Dan. Dan looked at us and the piece-of-shit mower and said, "Same problem?" We nodded in the affirmative. He said, "No problem", drained the gas out of the tank, and used a high-pressure air hose to clean the tank of debris. He said the Lawn-Boy blades act as a vacuum and sucks up the dirt and it gets into the motor; it happens all the time.

Roots and I thanked Dan and said, "How much?" He said, "Free; it only took 5 minutes to fix." After this, Walt would shadow us but not go into Dan's shop, as he knew he was not tolerated there.

Walt would blame "them," not him, for the clash of cultures, but more often than not, he would need to get us or his wife, June, to intercede, as some shop owners, restaurateurs and repairmen for some reason or another had a hard time tolerating Walt. In a usually subtle but visible way, they would give Roots and I a break, out of support or sometimes pity, but we appreciated it all the same.

Chapter 30
"You are Either Sick, Drunk or Crazy"

Walt had a variety of ways to make a point and drive home his view. Probably due to being a cop for over 20 years, he could generally read people well and use his instinct to his advantage. The advantage was rarely for money, but for most interpersonal relationships, especially close ones like family, he needed to hold all the power in that relationship.

Walt, as my brother and I also observed, saw June's mental and physical decline after re-settling in Florida. June reached more and more for, at first, Martinis, Gibson on the rocks, but later she was swigging gin out of teacups and finally just out of the bottle. Walt seemed to turn a blind eye to this except when dinner was burnt, or June passed out on the living room sofa at 4 pm, unable to get up.

One day, Walt exploded and told June that he had enough of her, as she was barely coherent and crying. He said, "June, you are either sick, drunk or crazy. If you are sick, admit yourself into a hospital. If you are drunk (which she was), then let's call the police and throw you into a "drunk tank" at the station; and if you are crazy, let's commit you to an insane asylum, where they will chain you to the wall!"

At other times, he would seem pleasant enough, but should he be shopping and an old man bump into him with a shopping trolley, he would say, "If you do this one more time, I will kick you in the cock." The anger of his tone and the reddening of his face indicated to the poor old man that he meant every word he said.

One memorable experience was that he wanted to try a new French restaurant, which opened in town. He liked that most restaurants had luncheon specials to attract customers. We drove in around 11:30 am, as Walt liked to eat early. We were the first customers at the restaurant that day. Imagine my chagrin when the sole waitress was the 16-year-old new French girl in my class, Gisèle. Her mother was the hostess, and presumably, the father was the chef.

Walt saw me turning red and knew that I knew the girl and vice-versa. Walt then said he was not interested in seeing a menu, that he wanted the daily special for two. He then started asking the waitress how much food was served in the special, and which portion was bigger: beef or chicken? The waitress was flustered, as Walt bombarded her with questions, and finally, her mother interceded and took control, which Walt did not seem to appreciate.

Walt sucked down the soup and devoured the bread that was served and kept asking for more bread. This happened three times and the hostess explained to Walt that usually only one plate of bread comes with the meal, and, as he wanted a fourth portion, there would be a small surcharge. Walt said, "Forget it," and waved the hostess away while adding in a loud voice, "This is the last time we will come here, as the place sucks and they overcharge."

The lunch arrived, but Walt felt it took too long and immediately complained about the lack of tenderness in the beef, though he devoured it all the same. I ate the chicken, which tasted fine, and secretly hoped we would get out without further incidents. As we finished up and Walt got the bill, the hostess came over and asked how the meal was. Walt's response was, "The food isn't fit for a pig." The hostess recoiled with surprise but regained her composure and said with a smile, "Please come back again and we will find you something that is."

This flew over Walt's head, and he left the restaurant but let out a loud and strung out a fart just before exiting the building. We never experienced what gourmet dish the hostess had planned for Walt's next visit.

Another unforgettable journey down memory lane was the time Walt took us to Tarpon Springs for dinner with the entire family. On that day, Walt was demonstrating to us about the art of being poor. The restaurant he chose was a local, average middle-class restaurant. As we ordered, he told us in front of the waitress that we needed to watch what we ordered and make sure it was not too expensive. As June ordered a fish dinner, he said, "We can't afford it." This set the tone for the rest of the meal, and when it was my turn, I wanted dinner with a side salad, which cost an extra twenty-five cents above the dinner price. Walt said that this was too expensive and we couldn't afford it. I took out a quarter and put it on the table and said, "Now we can afford it." This ramped Walt up and he said, "Why do you always make me into the asshole?" The waitress diplomatically retreated, and Walt went onto focusing on me as a "fat, smart-assed, four-eyed, greasy-haired, pimply-faced ingrate who will not amount to anything in life."

After the lovely meal, the evening ended with the waitress presenting the bill to Walt. If it amounted to 18 dollars and some change, Walt kept the dollar and left the change on the table. As it was customary at the time to pay waitstaff 15%, and they depended upon their tips to live on, the waitress was visibly upset, since she had been helpful and polite despite our behavior. She went to the manager, who took two dollars from her wallet to pay our waitress. Walt left the restaurant, both unaware and unconcerned about the incident.

Yet despite all this, Walt was still ramping up.

Chapter 31
"Psycho Cop"

Walt was highly strung in the early and mid-1970s, as he had a hard time adjusting to Florida and the new realities that he was no longer a cop. This fact made him more emotional and more resentful to all that was around him. As Roots and I integrated into Jr. High School and then High School, this seemed to heighten tension rather than create a more relaxed attitude, which we saw between our friends and their parents. Some of the outbreaks we witnessed at the time made my brother and I call Walt, "Psycho Cop."

I moved into my grandmother's former room after she was put into a nursing home full time. While on the surface this seemed good, Walt found it more and more important to come in to tell me to lower the volume of the stereo, or when all was quiet, to barge in to see what I was up to. After a while, I would lock the door to stop any casual intrusions. However, Walt did not take the hint.

When Walt went into a mouth-foaming rage, roughly two to three times a week, more often than not, I was the target for his attention. June would run to her room and cry, and drink gin, and Roots would do all that he could do to avoid Walt. Joey, the Airedale, also avoided Walt by always leaving the room Walt settled in to find a quieter, safer place to rest.

I was the oldest child and more often than not, foolishly or bravely, would on occasion push back against the nonsense, threats, rude comments, etc., that this angry man wanted to dish out. At this point in time, Walt behaved like a red cape was waved in front of a bull, and the fun began.

The stage is the ramp-up, which was very short and uniquely visible as his blood pressure rose and his fat face became red. At the same time, the beginning of his verbal escalation would include a warning, but usually, before the end of his sentence, you would be threatened physically. The midpoint of ramp-up was the profane verbal abuse. For me, it was typically, "You fat, four-eyed, pimply, piece of shit, I am going to kick the shit out of you!" For Roots, my brother, it was typically, "You little, weak, pimply-faced, piece of shit, I am going to beat the shit out of you!" For June, our mother, it was one of two, "You are either sick, drunk or crazy, you drunken slut!" or "You drunken slut, you stink like a bar rag!"

Next came phase three, which, I admit, I attracted 80 percent of the time, while Roots attracted it 20 percent of the time, and this was "Psycho Cop Rage," where he would get up and run after us. I would retreat to my bedroom first, and then he would huff and puff at my door. This usually was, "Open the door now, or I will kick it in! This is your last chance for you to take it like a man!" I would then go to the glass doors, which offered an exit or, in my case, an escape to the porch and out to the back yard. Walt would count, "One, two, three!!" He would then kick the door down, which was made from cheap pine, and he would pull the door frame with the force of his kick, and splinter the door, and enter the room in a full hateful rage. Meantime, I was out on the porch, exiting the door into the garden and slipping away. This infuriated him more, but being 50 plus in age, overweight, and already out of breath, he would stop, threaten, curse, and go back inside in the cool air-conditioned house.

Joey would then come out and make sure I was alright, and I would play with him in the yard or take him for a walk.

Roots was more clever than me, and when he was the focus of unbridled hate and rage, he usually slipped out the front door onto the street, and Walt could never catch him, as Roots was fast.

Another manifestation of Psycho Cop was driving rage. This is how that type of rage worked.

We would be driving, and something would usually happen externally that would set Walt off. One story we remember was that we pulled into a gas station one day in the piece-of-shit Austin Marina. He went to the rear gasoline tank and took the cap off and put it on the roof of the car. Walt filled the tank and closed the lid without remembering to put the cap back on the tank; it remained on the roof, and Roots and I did not notice it. As we exited from the gas station, a car pulled up behind us and tapped their horn two or three times. This set Walt off as he peered into the rearview window and yelled, "Go fuck yourself!" However, the car started to pull up next to us and again tapped their horn two or three times, which made Walt go apoplectic. He rolled down the car window and said, "You fucking pricks; I told you to go fuck yourselves!" About a hundred feet ahead was a red light, and the car very gingerly pulled up beside us. Walt was leering at them, and the veins in his neck were bulging. A young blond woman, about 20 years old, just slightly opened her window. Walt was ready to set off again, and then she said, "Sir, the cap of your gas tank is on the roof of your car, and you may want to get it before it falls onto the street." Walt downshifted emotionally, laughed, and said, "Thank you."

Another memory of Psycho Cop was when I was around 12 and succeeded with his help to build an F-4 Phantom jet model. Together, this took at least two weeks to accomplish, and he said to June that I did most of the work, which probably was not true, but I felt proud all the same. So far, so good. I added this to a small collection of model warships and monsters that I built, which were easier than this complicated and sophisticated jet. The night the jet was completed, I did something wrong, which triggered Walt. He came into the bedroom where my brother and I were sleeping, started whacking me as I scrambled and hid under the covers and used the pillow to lessen any head injuries he may cause. Roots just rolled into a ball and assumed a full bracing position under the covers. We knew, at that tender age, we had to do the best we could to protect ourselves, as Walt went from Dad to Psycho Cop. After taking admittedly cushioned whacks and listening to a string of abusive words, Walt then went to each of my models and smashed them onto the floor. The jet plane was resilient and received only minor damage, so Walt crushed it under his shoe.

I cried that night, not because of the hits or the words, but by breaking the model which we worked on together, Walt broke any remaining trust I had in him, and at this point, I made my emotion move from fearing to despising him.

However, with all the angst and turmoil, Roots and I could always find time to have a laugh at Walt's expense. The following story is a classic Walt encounter.

Chapter 32
"Walt, Does the Car Burn Oil?"

It started with Walt taking Joey to the park and all the usual dramatics of the new piece-of-shit Austin Marina flashing red and amber lights, grinding in the automatic transmission, and a bluish smoke coming out of the exhaust.

A few days before, Walt took Roots and me to a nearby used car dealer, which populated US 19 at the side of this deadly and forever under repair US highway. The night before, Walt acknowledged that the car was not fit for purpose, even though it was only two years old. He pulled into a used car lot and the owner and salesman came to the car. His unique sales proposal was that he was an honest used car salesman, as he was a Christian, and his name was Cliff, a forty-year-old bald, except with a few inches of short brown hair around the ears, tall, and average-shaped man, who looked every part of being a used car salesman. Walt told us, "Pucker up your assholes, as this guy will really try to screw us." Walt, without leaving the car, opened the window of this un-air-conditioned British pile of bolts slapped together by the diligent unions who plagued British Leyland in the mid-1970s.

Blue smoke, which earlier that morning was visible, now made it look as if the Austin Marina transformed itself into a British warship laying a thick smokescreen, as seen in an old film about the Battle of the Graf Spee, which took place off the coast of Argentina during World War II. The density of the smoke was virtually solid, and even Walt had a hard time restraining his cough.

Cliff asked Walt how old the car was, and Walt told him it was only two years old. He then asked how the car ran, and Walt said, "Like a dream." The next question was why Walt wanted to sell or trade it, and Walt told him that he needed the money; a white lie, but who doesn't need money? Finally, Cliff asked, "Does the car burn oil?" Now to understand the irony here, Roots and I were coughing from the poisonous fumes seeping into the car while Cliff used his handkerchief to filter out as much smoke as he could. Walt then said, "No, it doesn't burn oil." I wanted to gag as I watched Walt in order to see if he would laugh, but he put on a most serious face, and the tone of his voice made it clear to Roots and me that he was not fibbing, but lying for a reason. Cliff then said in between coughs, "What is your Christian name, sir?" Walt said, "Walt." Cliff followed by saying, "Walt, I am a Christian fellow, and I believe whatever people tell me, and maybe you did not hear my question due to all the traffic coming from US 19, so I will ask the question again. Walt, does the car burn oil?" Walt said with a straight face, "No." I pinched myself not to laugh but did let out a meek giggle while Roots did the same.

Cliff exhaled and coughed as he was being asphyxiated with the oil fumes of the malignant Austin Marina. Cliff said, "Walt, I will give you 200 dollars now for this car for scrap and parts." Now in Walt's mind, the car was worth something around 3,000 dollars give or take 500 dollars, but probably give. Walt concluded with a firm and slightly angry, "Fuck You!" He then put the car into low gear and surprisingly got enough traction to spin the wheels of this anemic, four-cylinder car, which spit sand, dirt, and gravel into Cliff's face.

As we drove away, we saw Cliff trying to exit the cloud of dust and noxious fumes, while Walt said, "Serves the cocksucker right." However, even Walt knew we had to fix the car, and, in my heart, I knew this would be my job next week, which would cause more friction with Walt.

The Austin Marina did provide unlimited laughs, as Walt came home one day and told us the story about how he lost a sale due to this "piece-of-shit car".

Chapter 33
Walt Falls for His Prospect - Literally

L ife with Walt in Florida was tough but not without unintended moments of levity, and, at times, hysterics. Walt could tell stories better than any living person I knew. He seemed to do it effortlessly and skillfully, and I always wondered if he had actually attempted to sell real estate, or anything else for that matter, he could have succeeded far above his wildest expectations. However, Walt had a union mentality, and, like one of his younger acquaintances once said on Mother's Day, "What is the absolute very least I can do for Mother and get away with it?" Walt lived by this motto, especially when it came to working in Florida Real Estate.

Some memorable Walt moments in history, which are still celebrated around the world with his living descendants, are as follows. Walt, in one of his later projects, was selling large one to five acre lots for larger homes near Tampa Airport. Instead of prospecting for new clients and working the phones or sending out brochures, Walt sat in a converted air-conditioned garage with an attached WC, and he waited for someone to pull into the driveway and ask him to show them site plans, or to visit a lot in the subdivision. This took place usually between the hours of 10 am and 3:30 pm, less an hour's lunch break. Walt called this "breaking his ass for a living." The funny thing is when the volatile Florida economy did well, Walt did well, and more often than not, the 1970s and 1980s economy did well indeed. "No pain but gain," was Walt's new motto.

We all remember that, one day, Walt had to get his favorite car, the Cutlass Supreme, worked on at the Oldsmobile garage. This meant he needed to take the piece-of-shit Austin Marina to work. Now, this crap car did not get attended to by the loving hands of mechanics trained by British Leyland. Walt used Bill-the-Hippy to cut costs, cut corners, and with spit, gum, and rubber bands keep this car operational. When Walt was feeling generous, he would call the 1974 Austin Marina "a foreign sports car," but, usually, he referred to it by the more accurate term of endearment, "that piece of shit." Well, this is what happened one day, a day that will live in infamy.

Walt drove the Austin to work. He hated it as much as we did, as the engine had no power and it did not have air conditioning. Even Joey hated it, as he was hot and smelly in the back on his way for a run; but I digress. Walt was spending the day watching a black and white TV in his office and simultaneously listening to country music on the AM radio. Walt joked to us that he could do two things at once. Around 3:30 pm, a car pulled into the driveway. Walt cursed under his bad breath and said, "Shit, now I have to stay late." Two middle-aged women pulled into the subdivision, unaware of Walt's unofficial work hours. They wanted to see a lot far away from the main road in order to have privacy. Walt showed them the site plan and tried to get rid of them by giving them a brochure and asking them to call tomorrow. The women pointed to the sign that showed office hours from 8:30 am until 6:30 pm, and said they drove from Lakeland to see this property. They politely but firmly asked Walt to see where the lot they liked was situated. Walt had no other option other than to take them in his Austin Marina.

Now the Austin had two front bucket seats and a tiny rear seat that could seat two medium-sized adults. It had four doors, but the women had trouble fitting into the back of the Austin. Walt helpfully pushed the driver seat and passenger seat forward to help them enter the rear of the car. So far, so good.

Once they confirmed their feet were now in the car, Walt closed the rear doors but found he could not fit into the driver's seat. Over the years, Walt blossomed from being six feet and 175 pounds to 235 pounds. His stomach protruded, and in this case, he could not literally get into the car. He knew one passenger was behind him, so he tilted the back of the seat to give him more room, as he could not push the entire seat back, as the woman's knees were up against the front seat. Walt had a very tight fit and used his legs to push the driver's seat back as it gave way under his weight and pressure. Just as he was about to squeeze into the car, the seat broke with Walt falling back, all 235 pounds onto the slender woman's legs. She let off a scream, which Walt said almost broke his eardrums. The seat collapsed and Walt was pinning the now hysterical woman's legs into a painful cramping position. The other woman was shocked and yelled, "Pull yourself off my sister, you beast!"

Walt then grabbed the steering wheel and used this to access all his weakening upper body strength to pull himself off the screaming woman behind him. As he inched upward, the hysteria reduced somewhat, as the woman started to feel relief from Walt's weight. Suddenly, however, the steering wheel, not designed for an obese man pulling on it, came off into Walt's hands, which sent the woman into another chorus of yells, screams of pain, and the sister joined in telling Walt to "Get up!"

Walt was back to square one, and grasping for the open window frame, took hold of this and slowly and not very gracefully extracted himself out of the car, left leg first, then his right leg, and, finally, he rolled onto the dirty pavement and on the ground in his crisp white shirt just to avoid the commotion of the distressed women in the car.

Walt said they did not walk but ran to their car and sped away. Needless to say, Walt didn't get this sale, and this was one of the gems which are told over and over again at every post-Walt family reunion.

As Roots and I graduated from university and moved away, we left the turmoil behind us. Yet, Roots would jokingly nudge me and tell me that, in fact, I liked and enjoyed the turmoil as I recalled a trip home to visit Walt and June at Disney World in Orlando.

Chapter 34
Walt Visits Disney World Florida

Walt never really mellowed, even as he approached 75 years old, and was repeatedly in and out of hospitals. While, on the occasional phone call and short visit, he could be pleasant, there was a storm brewing just under the surface, and, on occasion, it popped out. Walt succeeded in not only affecting my brother and me, but reached his grandson as well.

On one of my infrequent trips to see Mom and Dad, we always stayed away from the house I grew up in, as it brought back bad memories. I needed to get away from them to maintain a cordial relationship, as they were getting old. While this was a good strategy, it did not inoculate us from violent rage outbursts.

The first sign that Walt wasn't mellowing was when my family traveled from Europe to visit Disney in Orlando. We booked several nights in the Grand Floridian Hotel overlooking Lake Buena Vista. The plan was to pay for a room for Walt and June next to ours, and then they could spend evenings with their grandchildren at the theme parks. Boy, was this a mistake.

My first inkling things were not going to work out was after organizing a car for them and taking them from their home to the park 100 miles away. I asked how they liked their room, as they had a suite on the top floor. Walt said it was "Ehh," shrugging his shoulders. I said it should be great, not "Ehh." He then explained that, when they got to the room, they found it to be non-smoking, and they called up the front desk and demanded a smoking room. The only such room was one overlooking the restaurant and the car park. They traded my suite for this standard smoking room. Our mother, June, added, "You should know cigarettes are the only thing that bring me pleasure in life." She would die of lung cancer less than five years later.

Next, Walt found that Florida was hot in the evenings. As he had lived in Florida now for over thirty years, we thought he knew Florida was warm in the evenings. When we bought them a bottle of ice-cold water, Walt asked, "How much was that?" I said, "Two dollars." Walt said that Bob Eisner (the then CEO of Disney) was running a POW camp charging the paying guests two dollars to drink water in Florida.

Finally, on this trip, we had ordered a car to be delivered at the front of the resort after we checked out to take Walt and June back home. The bellman, a 20-year-old local college student, said that there were new instructions, and guests had to take a shuttle to the rental car office to collect their car. I protested and showed him the voucher that said the car would be delivered in front of the hotel reception area.

Walt heard us talking, and in the fastest ramp-up I ever saw, said, "You fucking lying cock-sucking four-eyed ballbusting piece of shit, get us the car now, fuck face!" The guy was almost in tears, probably never being called this by another human being before. To de-escalate the matter, I agreed to take the shuttle, but Walt couldn't resist yelling, "Fuck you and the rat," to the bellman as we left the crowded reception area.

Walt also had a couple of flare-ups with his oldest grandson. When the boy was five, he actually liked Walt and sat by him while Walt watched cable TV at home in Florida. Young Michael was amazed at the cable TV remote control and started pushing buttons. Walt said, "Stop that, please." Michael's fixation continued. "Stop it now." But Michael must have continued pushing buttons. Next thing, my wife and I heard a scream as Michael came running out of the family room into the living room, saying, "Grandpa wants to kill me!" Meanwhile, we saw Walt with a rolled-up newspaper yelling, "Come back here, you little bastard!"

At another time, Walt made an appointment for me to see his medical doctor for a prescription, when I had other plans for the day. When I met Walt at the infamous front door of his home to tell him I could not go to the doctor that afternoon, I was with my 5-year-old son. Walt let out a tirade calling me a useless, ungrateful fucker, and to get out as he never wanted to see me again. Michael, seeing Walt's contorted face, said, "Grandpa's making a monster face." With that, he told little Michael, "Beat it, you little bastard."

We stayed clear and away from Walt almost until the time of his death after that episode.

Chapter 35
The End of an Era or Error?

We were going to visit Florida with the family about two years later and heard from June that Walt was getting worse. I spoke with him very shortly on the phone, and he seemed mellow but a little frail. June asked us to visit and apologized for Walt's previous behavior. We said we would drop by the following week.

When we did drop by, June said Walt had been admitted to the hospital and was in a medically induced coma, as he was urinating blood and was in pain. She said that he woke up two nights before at 3 in the morning in pain and asked her to drive him to the hospital 10 miles away. She had been taking heavy-duty sleeping pills in order not to wake up in the night and was groggy. She then took some tranquilizers to calm her down before her nocturnal drive. She said she didn't remember actually driving him and only remembered arriving at the emergency room entrance. She added, "If we had been in an accident and killed, that would have been alright." I told her, "That may have been alright for you and Walt, but what about the innocent family of four you may have wiped out?" She was unrepentant and defiant.

The family and I went to the ward where Walt was situated. He had tubes down his throat and a catheter inserted to urinate. He also was on IVs. We were with him for thirty minutes. He seemed to know we were there but was unable to communicate. He grunted, growled and opened his eyes a few times. The nurse said he was not aware of us, but we felt he was almost trying to talk.

A humorous moment was when his two grandchildren started to spontaneously punch each other, which seemed to get him to move. The youngest grandson, Jamie, yelled, "Walt, wake up!" and he ever so briefly opened his eyes, rolled and closed them again.

I wonder what was going through his mind, or was he already gone? A day after this visit, we were told he passed away, just before his 80th birthday.

While preparing for his funeral, he had pre-ordered a headstone at the attractive veteran cemetery at Bay Pines. In an ironic moment, my mother said, "What should we put on his stone?" I said sarcastically, "Walt was loved and he loved." June thought that was a great idea, and Roots who was on the telephone said, "No way, Mom, this was a joke." Some meaningless line about resting in peace was finally agreed.

So, in the end, we go back to the beginning. Why these tales of The Walt? Because they are important. Collectively, all our tales and life adventures are worth remembering, but Walt had the potential for good, if not some degree of greatness. He could have been much more if he had desired. He chose the very least he could do and somehow knew that he let himself down and his family as well. He was above average in intelligence but wanted to coast rather than ride, and, as he got older, he was disappointed in the outcomes life presented due to his own choices. Yet, I wonder if he finally understood that it was not life, but Walt himself, that disappointed? As his oldest son, I knew in my heart that he could have been much more but chose to be so much less.

It is a bit ironic that Walt has taught me well, as in most of my own personal adventures, and that of Roots as well, if we were unsure of what we needed to do, we could ask, "What would Walt do?" Then do the opposite! This is not meant to be nasty, nor funny, as having a father, even a negative role model, is probably better than not having one at all. My wife, who lost her father at age five, would agree. She felt Walt showed me a flawed way forward and, usually, I moved through the maze by doing the opposite of what he would do.

What next, I wonder, as Roots does. What about our children and grandchildren? How will they thrive in this very uncertain and, at times, frightening environment that we live in? Will we be role models or negative role models for them? I hope the former, but if the latter, and if it helps them go forward, then it is a win-win for us all.

By this logic, I hope Walt did find the peace that eluded him in life, and, wherever he is, that he finds the contentment that Roots and I have found our way - a much different and I think better way than he originally intended. Finally, for a moment, let's be positive and hope that the younger detective, Walt of the 1950s, has won the internal fight and his spirit and energy remain rather than the destructive and troubled Psycho Cop of the 1970s.

June passed away of lung cancer two years after Walt; she was 79. Both Walt and June are buried in a Veteran's Administration Cemetery in West Florida. The area they have been interned is on a small hill overlooking the Boca Ciega Bay. Roots and I smiled and noted that this small real estate acquisition by Walt and June, the beauty and tranquility of the cemetery, was one of the best decisions they made in their later years.

Good luck to you, June, and you also, Walt. Roots and I forgive you both for the past but refuse to forget; therefore, we hope that future generations will learn from these "Tales of The Walt."

- The End

Acknowledgements

I want to thank the following people for helping me put this book together in order to help make Walt come to life.

- Eiko Merlino - Illustration and cover design
- Michael Merlino - Publishing
- Sandra Marie - Executive Editor
- Tom Skinner - Contributor
- Warren Merlino - Contributor
- James-Paul Merlino - Contributor
- Cheryl Merlino - Contributor
- Pippa Michalski - Contributor

To see more from the author, please visit

https://paulmerlinoauthor.com/